Journey
of a
Strong-
Willed
Child

Journey of a Strong-Willed Child

Kendra Smiley
with Dr. Aaron Smiley
and John Smiley
(the resident dad)

MOODY PUBLISHERS
CHICAGO

All Scripture quotations, unless otherwise indicated, are taken from the *Holy Bible, New International Version*®. NIV®. Copyright © 1973, 1978, 1984 by International Bible Society. Used by permission of Zondervan Publishing House. All rights reserved.

Cover Design and Illustrations: Garborg Design Works, Inc.
Interior Design: LeftCoast Design
Editor: Ali Childers

Library of Congress Cataloging-in-Publication Data

Smiley, Kendra, 1952-
    Journey of a strong-willed child / by Kendra Smiley, with Dr. Aaron Smiley and
John Smiley.
        p. cm.
    Includes bibliographical references.
    ISBN: 978-0-8024-4353-3
        1. Child rearing—Religious aspects—Christianity. 2. Control (Psychology)
in children. 3. Smiley, Aaron, 1981- I. Smiley, Aaron, 1981- II. Title.

BV4529.S477 2004
248.8'45—dc22
2003024377

We hope you enjoy this book from Moody Publishers. Our goal is to provide high-quality, thought-provoking books and products that connect truth to your real needs and challenges. For more information on other books and products written and produced from a biblical perspective, go to www.moodypublishers.com or write to:

Moody Publishers
820 N. LaSalle Boulevard
Chicago, IL 60610

3 5 7 9 10 8 6 4 2

Printed in the United States of America

*This book is dedicated
to the strong-willed children
whose parents love them enough
to maintain loving control.*

Contents

Acknowledgments

There are many people who deserve a thank-you when it comes to the writing of this book.

John and I would like to thank:

- Our dear friend and former office manager, Pam Rush, who made every project so much easier.
- Our extended family (near and far), who have encouraged us as they have encouraged our children (strong-willed or otherwise).
- Our Moody Publishers editors, Elsa Mazon, Ali Childers, and Betsey Newnhuyse, whose enthusiasm and prayers were and are a wonderful blessing.
- Our son Aaron, for being so transparent and so honest.
- The remainder of our children and children-in-law: Matthew and Marissa, Kristin, and Jonathan and Ashley for being the supportive, creative, and delightful people that they are. We are blessed.
- And neither last nor least, my very best friend, Jesus.

Your turn, Aaron.

Thanks to:
- My first grade teacher, Grandma, who taught me how to read and expected the best out of me every day. Thanks, too, for always finding something for me to eat and for sharing memories with me.
- Mrs. Janet Crouch for caring about me as a person first and a student second.
- Mrs. Ada Murray for her discipline that made our class feel so safe.
- Mrs. Marty Lindvahl for her forgiveness and for never keeping score.
- Mr. Mark Lindvahl for modeling excellence day in and day out.
- Mr. Bill Medler for challenging me to learn how to think.
- Mr. Quentin Ryder for allowing me the freedom to express myself and to share my ideas.
- Ed Lockhart for trusting me with adult responsibility at such a young age.
- Lawrence and Loretta Alt for talking and dreaming with me when I was a boy, but treating me like an adult. Thanks for encouraging me when it seemed like no one but my family believed in me.
- Uncle Wynn for all the effort he put into being an uncle. That effort provided *all of us* with many great experiences.
- Grandpa for giving me the opportunity to be a part of agriculture, an interest that means so much to me, and for being generous in every way.
- Mom for putting my ideas and memories of childhood into this book so that they can help others. Thanks for crying and laughing with me through the ups and downs.
- Dad for never giving up hope that I would finish my journey and for the rules that were reasonable and never changed on a whim. Thanks for the fair punishment. You had the hardest job because you put limits on my life that I hated but didn't want to live without.
- Matthew, my older brother, for sharing his friends with me and including me. Thanks for always being a rational voice in my sometimes irrational world.

- Jonathan, my younger brother, for being so flexible and being willing to play with me when we were younger and later helping me with all the different work we've done together.
- Kristin, my wife, whom I do not deserve but who is a blessing from God. Thanks for caring for me and loving me through my ups and downs. Your love helps to make my life complete.
- Jesus Christ, for saving me from my sins. I will never fully understand why He sacrificed so much for us, but I gratefully accept His free gift of salvation.

Introduction:
Aaron and Others

*The Lord your God has blessed you
in all the work of your hands.
He has watched over your journey
through this vast desert.*
DEUTERONOMY 2:7

"Aaron wants two cookies," said Matthew, his older brother. "He wants a glass of cold milk, too." Once again, Matthew was correct. Aaron was content to allow his older brother to speak for him for the first eighteen months or so of his life. And why not? He was doing a great job of getting Aaron just what he wanted. Who would have ever suspected that this quiet little guy would be our strong-willed child? Yet, we had an inkling from early on.

"No! Again!" Aaron said in loud, defiant protest as I calmly explained that our time on the amusement ride had come to a close. "NO!" he said even louder, with fast and furious tears. "AGAIN!"

As I pried his little fingers from the safety bar, another rendition of "It's a Small World" played in our ears. I won the battle, but I had a very unhappy young man on my hands. He wanted to go again, and it was obvious that he felt certain that he should have what he wanted. Generally speaking, what Aaron wanted was to be in control of himself. That's what your strong-willed child wants, too! It's not just Aaron, it's Aaron and others.

It has been said that a journey begins with a single step. Many times the journey of a strong-willed child starts even before the first step is taken. A strong-willed child, it would seem, is born strong-willed, with intense opinions and a demanding nature. He's born with the desire to control his own destiny and the uncanny ability to actually secure that control in many instances. Strong-willed children come into the world strong-willed and, for that matter, probably exit as strong-willed adults. By that time they have potentially tempered the negative aspects of their strong-willed nature. They have learned to cooperate, acquiesce, and respond to the leadership of others when it is in their best interest. In all hopes, they also capitalize on the pluses of their strong-willed nature. That is the goal we have for our high-maintenance children. Our desire is to contribute in a positive way to their development as responsible adults. Our job is not to break their spirit, but to shape their will.

This is not an easy job. Actually, parenting *any* child is challenging, but a strong-willed child adds a dimension not found in raising a more compliant child. I know that my husband, John, and I were blessed with a 100 percent, genuine, certifiable strong-willed child. And this child was recognized as such, almost immediately, by his father—a strong-willed child turned responsible, loving, cooperative adult. This father-son combination provided me valuable insight and ultimately gave each one of us—mom, dad, and son—the motivation and understanding we needed to write this book. You'll find encouragement and instruction through this description of one strong-willed child's journey.

The journey of your strong-willed child will not be precisely like Aaron's, but undoubtedly it will be a journey with bumps and curves and perhaps even an occasional detour. It is our hope that Aaron's journey will help you realize that (1) you are not alone, (2) the strong-willed child has thought and behavior patterns that can be understood and anticipated, and (3) there are insights and strategies that can help you and your child on the journey. It can sometimes seem like a passage through a long, dark tunnel, but there is hope, not just for survival but also for success, as measured by the emergence of a responsible adult with godly character.

Before we begin our journey, it is essential to establish the definition we will use for a strong-willed child. Dr. James Dobson, largely respected as an expert on this topic, wrote that a strong-willed child "seems to be born with a clear idea of how he (or she) wants the world to be operated and an intolerance for those who disagree."[1]

That generally summarizes the strong-willed child's black-and-white thinking and intolerance. We can add a few more qualifiers to that definition. A strong-willed child *appears* confident. A strong-willed child can be both charming and defiant. He is *very* persistent and is even willing to take punishment to win. A strong-willed child is generally gifted in manipulation. In fact, he is able and willing to cause emotional upset if it is a means to gain control of his life. A strong-willed child does not necessarily want to control everyone else; he simply does not want to be controlled. Yet, he will strive to control someone threatening to control him. Who is that typically? That's right! It's you, his loving parent. His parent who might be wondering why this child is so difficult and so opinionated—so "right" all the time.

> *"He that complies against his will, is of his own opinion still."*[2]
> BUTLER

If a strong-willed child is one who knows how he wants the world to operate and is intolerant of those who disagree, what is he NOT? Are there behaviors that are sometimes misinterpreted as strong-willed? Absolutely! My mother used to say that her children were not stubborn; they merely had "exceptional resolve." Yes, we did, but we were not strong-willed. We were stubborn—oops, sorry, Mom—I mean we had exceptional resolve, but there were very few issues that I was willing to go to the mat for. That is in contrast to a strong-willed child, who many times chooses fighting and punishment over acquiescence. Being strong-willed goes well beyond being stubborn. A strong-willed child resolutely defends his position and questions any and all authority over him to determine his or her "right" to retain command. That is more than stubborn.

> *The rod of correction imparts wisdom,*
> *but a child left to himself disgraces his mother.*
> PROVERBS 29:15

Sometimes undisciplined children are mistakenly labeled as strong-willed. A child who has managed to gain control over the adults in his life may or may not be strong-willed. Remember, a strong-willed child's goal is not to control everyone else. Instead it is to maintain control over himself (even though some adult is clamoring for that control). A bright child who has determined how to outwit his loving (though unprepared) parent might repeatedly "get his way" and make others miserable when he does not get it. But this lack of parental discipline does not confirm a strong-willed child. It merely encourages inappropriate behavior. **Warning: Lack of discipline can, however, encourage, reinforce, and empower a true strong-willed child to even greater heights (or should I say depths?) of poor behavior.

A strong-willed child is not bad or stupid or mean, although he may be classified as such by others who do not understand or appreciate his positive attributes.

Even a child is known by his actions,
by whether his conduct is pure and right.
PROVERBS 20:11

Do you have a strong-willed child? For practical purposes, I will refer to the strong-willed child in the male gender. This is not to imply that only boys are strong-willed. In my findings, I discovered almost an equal number of boys and girls classified by their parents as strong-willed. Furthermore, the strong-willed child is not of any particular birth order. Our strong-willed son is our second child. Yours may be your youngest child or maybe a firstborn or an only child. I have also discovered that strong-willed children do not have only one personality type. (See Tim LaHaye's *Spirit-Controlled Temperament*[3] or Florence Littauer's *Personality Plus*[4] for a discussion of personalities.) Persons with the choleric personality type are described as thinking they are "always right," and I have definitely known of strong-willed children in that category. However, there are girls and boys who are choleric in their nature and are not strong-willed. My husband, the former strong-willed child, is predominantly phlegmatic in personality (having a quiet will of iron). Therefore, personality type does not guarantee or disqualify someone as a strong-willed child. A strong-willed child can be male or female, oldest, middle, or youngest, and have any personality profile. There are similarities but no carbon copies. Do you have a strong-willed child?

And do not forget to do good and to share with others,
for with such sacrifices God is pleased.
HEBREWS 13:16

The phone rang, and it was a good friend on the line. "Do you think we might be able to drive down to visit you on our way to Indianapolis for Easter break?" the caller inquired. "There are two reasons for our visit. Number one, you once told me that your son Aaron was a strong-willed child, and it looks as though we've been blessed with one, too. It's hard to believe that your respectful college-age son was once a strong-willed child. And it's equally hard to believe that our iron-willed twelve-year-old will ever turn out to be a respectful college student! And, number two, this same son recently announced that he wanted to grow up to be a farmer and a pilot, and the *only* person we know with that career combination is John. If we can stop by, maybe John can convince Nate that to farm and fly he must pass seventh grade. Then perhaps Nate can go and play, and we can pick your brains about your experience as parents of a strong-willed child."

I welcomed our friends to our home. After John spent time talking with Nathan about the rewards and requirements of his chosen career fields, the adults settled down for a discussion about parenting a strong-willed child. Our conversation had just begun when, to our surprise, our strong-willed child turned young adult, Aaron, arrived at home from college a day early for Easter break. As soon as he realized the topic of our conversation, he entered into it with enthusiasm. I sat in awe as I witnessed his ministry to our guests.

"I don't know what Nate was thinking when he pushed the issue with his science teacher," lamented his father.

"I know *just* what he was thinking," Aaron replied. And he went on to describe the thought process of a strong-willed child who has declared war on an unsuspecting adult perceived as either vulnerable or deserving of the treatment.

Nathan's dad sat in wonder. Could there be another human on this earth who not only understood his son's behavior but also declared it predictable? Was it possible that his son was not an anomaly, a quirk of nature? Did this child respond and react in a certain way because of how God created him and not just to frustrate and annoy his parents?

As Aaron recounted story after story (some familiar, some shockingly new to me), I saw a look of hope in our friends' eyes. Hearing the struggles and successes in Aaron's journey as a strong-willed child gave these parents hope. Hearing the insights and actions that helped us navigate his

journey gave them tools. Hearing about the people whose behavior positively influenced Aaron gave them new vision, suggestions, and solutions
to help Nathan grow into confident manhood.

A Closer Look with Aaron

I remember the day when I came into the family room
and found the adults gathered there discussing strong-willed
children. Ah, I thought, now this is one topic that I truly
understand. My biggest surprise was to realize that our visi-
tors thought their son, their strong-willed child, had some
sort of problem—that he was somehow diabolical or targeting
them out of meanness. Meanness? The only difficulty I could
imagine was that Nathan was a very strong-willed guy. I started
to tell some of my own horror stories of wanting to have control, and Nathan's parents, especially his dad, were amazed
that I had one or two that outdid their son's. Nate started
looking better and better to his folks thanks to some of my
antics as a strong-willed child. And when I could actually finish a story that Nathan's dad started, "guessing" with great
accuracy what had happened next in the particular battle, I
was sure that the visiting parents were going to declare me a
genius! Was I? Am I? No. (Both of my brothers got higher
ACT scores than I did, although my mom thinks I'm pretty
smart!) What I am is an adult who was a strong-willed child
not too long ago. I realized that day that I could help parents
like Nathan's learn how to appreciate and handle their strong-
willed child.

And thus the idea was born. Aaron traveled the bumpy road of a
strong-willed child, and we, his parents, were with him along the way.
The trip was not always an easy one for him or us, but the destination
made the journey worthwhile. Luke opened his written account of
Jesus' life with these words, "Therefore, since I myself have carefully

investigated everything from the beginning, it seemed good also to me to write an orderly account for you . . ." And that is precisely what we have tried to do. Throughout this book you'll hear our stories and those of others. Join us as we take you down the road we've traveled. Join us on the *Journey of a Strong-Willed Child*.

"When the train goes through a tunnel and the world gets dark, do you jump out? Of course not, you sit still and trust the engineer to get you through."[5]

CORRIE TEN BOOM

CHAPTER ONE

The Journey Begins:
Birth to Pre-Kindergarten

For you created my inmost being;
you knit me together in my mother's womb.
I praise you because I am
fearfully and wonderfully made;
your works are wonderful, I know that full well.
PSALM 139:13–14

Our strong-willed child, Aaron Joseph Smiley, arrived in February of 1981. I still remember the moment of his birth. Dr. Tanner (our family physician and the father of five sons) announced, "It's a boy!"

Naively, my enthusiastic response was, "Oh good! I already know how to *do* boys!" I don't remember seeing Dr. Tanner's eyes roll to the back of his head, but undoubtedly he wondered how I could make such a ridiculous statement!

Our first son, Matthew, was two years old at the time. I would classify him as a compliant child. It was not that he always obeyed us perfectly, but he did "aim to please." As a former teacher, I had perfected the "schoolteacher look." You know how it goes: lips drawn tightly in a pseudo-pucker, eyebrows knit together, and a very stern countenance. That "look" was completely effective with my oldest son. A stern look or a gentle scolding generally brought about conviction, legitimate repentance, and a heartfelt vow to "do better." (Can you see why I had such confidence when son number two was born? Just look at how well I had been doing with son number one!)

But the truth was that I did not know how to "do boys" any more than I had conquered the art of parenting. And that was a truth that I was soon to discover. Forget "the look" when it came to Aaron.

"Liam, my four-year-old and I were driving home from preschool, and he asked if we could have lunch at McDonald's. I explained that it wasn't a possibility. Because Liam is strong-willed (and not to be deterred by such a flimsy statement), he pursued the idea with great determination. When I finally convinced him that I was NOT going to stop at the fast-food restaurant for lunch, Liam folded his arms across his chest and humphed, 'Well, Mommy, you are making a bad choice.' My own words, frequently spoken, were repeated in an effort to manipulate me with guilt and gain control."

While Matthew was compliant and aimed to please, Aaron had different ideas. I used to explain his strong-willed nature this way: "If we draw a line in the sand and tell Aaron not to cross it and why, *and* we tell him the penalty for disobedience, he will immediately step up to the line, as close as he can possibly get, and inquire, 'What did you say you were going to do to me if I step over this line?' Then he reviews the consequences and determines whether or not to cross the line. And many times, over the line he goes." Ah, a strong-willed child.

Aaron did not always use defiance to try to get his way. This sweet little boy came into the world looking just like the Gerber baby, complete with wispy blond hair, big blue eyes, and a ready smile. One of my earliest recollections of his manipulation skills involved the use of charm, not defiance. When he was just a little over two years old, I remember scolding Aaron. I don't recall the issue, but I do remember his actions. When I finally paused in my reprimand and took a breath, Aaron smiled his deep-dimpled smile, reached out with his chubby little hands and patted me gently on both cheeks. "Dat be alwight, Mommy," he cooed in an effort to comfort me, his overwrought mother. Ah, what a sweet, caring child. Wait a minute! I wasn't the one in need of comfort. I wasn't the one in trouble, he was! I'm sure Aaron thought, "If this works, why not go for it?"

"Christine did not want to go to the first day of pre-school. I talked her into getting into the truck, and then she was all excited and really wanted to go. We got there, and all of a sudden, she was mad—screaming, crying, absolutely mad—and she could not believe that I was going to make her go into this lady's room. So she would not go, would not go, would not go. 'Mom, I hate that lady, don't make me go, don't make me go. I can't believe you're doing this to me. I don't want to go, she's mean, she's mean, she's mean! I hate that lady. I hate that lady 'cause she hates me. Take me home right now!'"

Strong emotion can definitely sway a parent. "I can't believe you're doing this to me" can make any parent step back and think. Hopefully, the parent filters this sentiment through the mind to realize that strong emotion and words like "mean" and "hate" are words used to manipulate and gain control. Also, strong emotion can translate into a tantrum, which can add the term "embarrassment" to your list of sentiments.

Very few tricks that Aaron tried (charm, guilt, strong emotion, or otherwise) worked with his dad. Remember, I told you that John is a strong-willed child turned responsible adult.

> *"It is a wise father that knows his own child."*[1]
> SHAKESPEARE

He knew the tricks and the importance of wise parenting.

At one point, John and two-year-old Aaron were literally eyeball-to-eyeball on the stairs, and the words from John's mouth were as follows: "Aaron, you will not win. When I tell you to do something, you must do it." If only that was the last time he had to make that statement! Even at an early age, Aaron desired control of his world.

"On another occasion, Emily was sitting at the table doing a craft project with her dad, and she told him out of the blue that he was a genius. Her dad asked her why, and she said, 'because you do everything I say.' Emily was three-and-a-half when this happened."

Aaron accepted Christ as his Savior at around four years old. It was actually the result of the guilt and remorse he felt about his own out-of-control, strong-willed behavior. He was having a very bad day and was in trouble with everyone in the family—Dad, Mom, and his older brother.

Here is a little background. Beginning when he was a toddler, Aaron was interested in agriculture and animals. I remember pulling into a cornfield on one of the family farms and hearing little Aaron pipe up from the backseat, "Dat torn looks dood!" (Translation: That corn looks good!) Our older son did not notice the status of the corn and had no opinion about its potential yield. Aaron's paternal grandfather is a farmer. This common love of agriculture made these two fast friends from the very beginning.

Now, back to the story of Aaron's personal encounter with Christ. As I said previously, that day he was behaving quite poorly (gross understatement). Bedtime finally came, and with it, the hope for a better tomorrow with less confrontation. Finally, there was peace and quiet. The next morning Aaron was up quite early. He waddled down the stairs in his footie pajamas, dragging one of his favorite blankets. When he arrived at the threshold of the kitchen, he stopped abruptly, waited for my attention, and then proceeded with his announcement.

"I asked Jesus into my heart last night," he declared. I was thrilled about this and immediately began to ask him about the details.

"That is just great!! Tell me all about it," I pried. "What happened to help you make this decision?"

"Well," he began, "I was soooooooo bad yesterday that everyone was mad at me. I figured that even *Grandpa* would have been mad."

(Remember, as far as Aaron was concerned, he and Grandpa were as tight as you could get. So the thought of Grandpa being mad was a very serious thing!)

He continued, "But I knew that even if everyone else was mad at me, Jesus loved me, so I asked Him into my heart."

By the way, that conversion experience was real and is often referred to by Aaron as "the most boring testimony possible." Personally I call it "the testimony every mother wants her child to have." Understanding God's love was important and would temper Aaron's behavior somewhat, but it definitely did not turn him into a compliant child.

You have made known to me the path of life;
you will fill me with joy in your presence,
with eternal pleasures at your right hand.
PSALM 16:11

The same year, Aaron became a big brother. This event was exciting for everyone in the family. And Aaron was no exception. I can still picture his little face tightening up with excitement and hear him say, "I love Jonathan so much—I just want to squeeze his guts out!" The fact that everyone else in the family thought that he just might do that very thing was a little scary. But we kept a cautious eye on the baby and Aaron and watched as the little strong-willed child assumed the role of nurturing big brother.

And he has given us this command:
Whoever loves God must also love his brother.
1 JOHN 4:21

A Closer Look with Aaron

My earliest memory of being a strong-willed child and having an intense desire to be in charge of my own life was when I was four years old. We bought a small house in town and proceeded to tear down our old farmhouse in order to build a new home on that location. Even though Matthew and I were little, there were things we did to help my dad with his project. Because there were raw materials in the old house that could be utilized in our new one, he was literally tearing the house down rather than burning it. One of our jobs was to sort various building supplies, like hardwood, from the useless things, like shingles.

One day we were carrying materials from one pile to another. It goes without saying that this was a silly job. As a four-year-old, I could see little importance in simply reorganizing the junk! And if such a stupid job really was legitimate, for goodness' sake, let's get a tractor going to at least make the task easier and more fun. I made that suggestion, and it fell on deaf ears. Dad, for some reason—probably because a tractor was really not necessary—said that our work assignment was NOT going to change.

If there is one thing a strong-willed child dislikes, it is doing any task or assignment that he deems useless—especially if he suggested a "better way" to do the meaningless job, and it was rejected. And on that particular day, that is precisely what happened! I wanted my idea to be honestly considered. Using a tractor made complete sense to me. I wanted to defend my position, but I wasn't given that opportunity.

My older brother might have thought the sorting job was a bad idea too, and he may even have liked my idea to use a tractor; but he didn't choose to cause a problem. I did. I simply decided that I would not do what Dad had ordered and expected. Dad would have to pay the price for not considering my great idea. I wouldn't work as hard as he wanted me to, and he would have to shift some of his attention to me and away from his agenda. I remember Matthew telling me that my slowdown strike was a bad idea. When Dad noticed my manipulation of the situation, slowing down but not completely disobeying (a gentle way to say defiance under control), he told me precisely what I was supposed to do, and he also told me the consequences for disobedience. I would be paddled. I pondered my options, much to my brother's discomfort. "You better do it, Aaron," he said. "Dad's serious!" I knew that he was serious, but I had to decide if my work slowdown, impeding Dad's progress, was more important than the pain I'd receive. And, guess what? I decided to go for the paddling.

As I cried, Dad announced that he expected me to do as I was told. As you may guess, I weighed the pros and cons of another confrontation. My brother (the compliant one) by now determined that I needed my head examined. "Come on, Aaron, do what you're supposed to do." He could not fathom the thought that winning my case was so important that I would pay a price. That was the first time, but not the last, that I realized we were wired differently. He couldn't understand my strong-willed nature, and I couldn't understand why he couldn't understand. (But I did appreciate his sympathy when I decided to go for a second round before my Dad was able to make his point that defiance would not win.)

> *Your word is a lamp to my feet*
> *and a light for my path.*
> PSALM 119:105

A Good Word from John, the Resident Dad

I can still remember hearing Kendra say in exasperation, "Parenting a strong-willed child is just like parenting any other child . . . TIMES TEN!" There is truth in that statement on two fronts. All kids need the love of their parents. And parents want their children to grow up to be responsible adults. Furthermore, Christian parents hope that their kids will learn to love and obey God. Those similarities are true whether you have been blessed with a strong-willed child or not.

The other truth in Kendra's frustrated exclamation is that the day-to-day task of parenting a strong-willed child is definitely a more exhausting job. There is very little rest and reprieve when you are the parent of a strong-willed child under the age of five. Your responsibility to provide love and to guide their journey to responsible adulthood is more challenging than the job of the parent of a compliant child, yet it is no less rewarding.

As an Air Force Reserve pilot, there were times when I was away from home. At one point, I flew a mission to Germany and remained there for ten days. That was when Aaron, only three years old at the time, decided to take advantage of Kendra's single-mom status and her recent introduction into the nature of a strong-willed child. I called home to see how things were going and discovered one very distraught mom! My recollection is that the entire phone call involved Kendra crying and me listening to Kendra crying. I knew that something had to be done when I arrived back home.

I took Aaron aside and explained to him that "Mom and I are one. When you upset Mom, you upset me. And when you upset me, you will have to pay the price." Aaron understood that there would be negative ramifications. (There will be more on those negative ramifications/discipline in the next chapter.) He understood that Kendra and I were in this parenting thing together and that I would not allow him to harass her. Whenever necessary, I would protect Kendra (the parent just learning about the tenacity of a strong-willed child).

Appreciating the blessing of a strong-willed child may be difficult at times. But don't get discouraged or give up. Galatians 6:9: *Let us not become weary in doing good, for at the proper time we will reap a harvest if we do not give up.* The "proper time" may not be today or tomorrow. But today is the time to begin to develop the skills you will need to parent your strong-willed child.

If Kendra was even close with her "TIMES ten" claim, you have no time to waste.

By the time Aaron reached school age, there was no doubt in my mind that Aaron was a high-maintenance child. In my thinking, that title "high-maintenance" put most of the responsibility on us as parents. We didn't have a label or an excuse for behavior that needed to be corrected. Just as a fine-tuned race car demands more sophisticated and time-consuming maintenance, I realized that our potential "top performer" demanded more sophisticated (read: frequent and intense) effort. As he prepared to go to the adventure called school, I prayed that the adults who would have his attention for the majority of the day would appreciate his attributes, keep him under control, and help to mold and nurture his development.

Because John and I are both teachers by training, we instilled in Aaron a respect for education and the teaching profession. He also knew that we would reinforce any discipline administered in school. It was our hope that the teachers would care about Aaron enough to control and encourage him. Some did, some did not.

CHAPTER TWO

Avoiding the Discipline Detour

*My son, do not despise the Lord's
discipline and do not resent his rebuke,
because the Lord disciplines those he loves,
as a father the son he delights in.*
PROVERBS 3:11–12

The responsibility of disciplining a strong-willed child is by far one of the largest potential detours in the journey. Over and over again the question arises, "Does a two-year-old really need discipline?" The question in return is, "Does your two-year-old choose to defy you?" And if the answer is "yes," that is also the answer to question number one. The time to begin to discipline or train your child is not based on a chronological date or stage, but it is based on the individual development and needs of your child.

I knew a young couple that announced from the beginning of their daughter's life that they were not going to discipline her until she was able to talk. To them, words would indicate understanding on the part of their child, and that was the guideline they established. Although their daughter was still not talking at eighteen months old, they continued with their strategy: "no discipline until Mandi is able to talk to us." Mandi was no dummy, and I watched her get by with some pretty defiant behavior while keeping her mouth shut. In fact, it is my theory (never to be proven or disproved) that Mandi was capable of talking long before she finally uttered her first words. She *knew* that sooner or later she would talk, and the jig would be up. Then her parents would go to "part two" of the program and begin to discipline her. She held out as long as she could, until around the age of two as I recall, and then she gave in. If Mandi was a strong-willed child like Aaron, she might still be silent today! A certain age or stage is not necessarily the perfect indicator of when discipline should begin. You need to discipline your child when he chooses to defy you. And there is usually little doubt when a strong-willed child chooses defiance.

O Lord, do not rebuke me in your anger
or discipline me in your wrath.
Psalm 6:1

Disciplining a strong-willed child can be frustrating. The ability of a young strong-willed child to keep arguing when most adults are exhausted often leads to the incorrect conclusion that discipline does not work. Again, that is an *incorrect conclusion*. But in order to see the benefits of loving discipline, there are some very important "Rules of the Road" for disciplining children. First of all, discipline should NEVER be done in anger. When you do this, you have lost control. The reason you are disciplining your child is to control his wayward behavior and to teach him correct behavior. An out-of-control adult is not effective and is actually counterproductive.

There were times when I found myself angry because of the behavior of Aaron. At that point, I left the room to regain my composure and returned to administer the appropriate discipline. Did I always do that? No, and my older sons developed a stand-up comedy routine based on me swinging my arm wildly into the backseat of our car, hoping to connect with one of them and stop their fighting, arguing, complaining— any or all of the above. In those instances, I was attempting to control my children's behavior when I wasn't even successful at controlling my own. That goofiness did NOTHING to gain control of the poor behavior (except maybe distract them as they dodged and giggled at my ridiculous actions). That was not discipline—it was slapstick comedy with the potential to cause an automobile accident.

There are two more important points to be considered in the discipline of a strong-willed child of any age. Number one, you must pick your battles wisely. If you chose to, you could fight all day with a strong-willed child and exasperate your child. What is really important? Not a bad question to ask yourself.

I was doing a book signing in a major metropolitan area, and a young woman came into the store with her toddler in a stroller. The two-year-old was wearing a biking helmet and my first thought was, "My goodness, this mom must be a very poor stroller driver!" As she made it to the front of the line, she pointed down at her little darling and said, "He wanted to wear it, and I decided it wasn't worth a fight." How true! (And how wise.)

"The main thing is to keep the main thing the main thing."

UNKNOWN

When Aaron and Matthew were just twenty-one months and four years old, respectively, the family made a very long trip by car to California. My husband, John, an Air Force Reserve pilot, was scheduled for some additional flight training, and the reporting time was not negotiable. We loaded the kids into our sedan and started on a fifty-two-hour road trip. In order to maintain peace and harmony, we planned to do as much traveling around-the-clock as we could, and I organized many diversions for the boys. I hung men's shirts on the hooks by each of their seats. The bottom hems were sewn shut. Inside the shirts-turned-bags were all sorts of goodies, including metal cookie sheets that were used for desktops and magnetic playing boards. I wrapped up little toys and markers (each individually packaged) as well as magnetic letters and shapes. Every waking hour each boy was given a new package to unwrap. Believe it or not, this kept the boys happy during the trip.

After we were in the car for about thirty-six hours, we decided to stop at a restaurant rather than eat another of the lunches I packed. The boys enjoyed their meal, and then we allowed them to run around the area in which we were seated. There were no other patrons close enough to be bothered by their footloose behavior, although I'm sure some wondered why any parent in his right mind would allow such commotion. We decided that corralling them was not a battle we wanted to fight. After all, they would soon be corralled for the remainder of the trip, still some sixteen hours. What battles do you want to fight?

No discipline seems pleasant at the time, but painful.
Later on, however, it produces a harvest of righteousness and peace
for those who have been trained by it.
HEBREWS 12:11

The next important point is this: the battles that you choose to fight, you must win. Remember what John said to Aaron during their eyeball-to-eyeball meeting on the stairs? "You will not win." Did Aaron believe him? Maybe not that day. Did he eventually believe him? Yes. When you pick a battle, you must win. That is why you don't want to engage in every possible skirmish.

A man reaps what he sows.
GALATIANS 6:7

As soon as he can reason, a strong-willed child wants to know the consequences that will result from his misbehavior. Aaron got as close to "the line" as he could to weigh the joy of control against the pain of the consequences before choosing whether or not to cross the line. That is knowledge every strong-willed child desires. When you are determining the consequences, NEVER make a threat you cannot keep. The mother who shrieks, "If you do that you'll be grounded for life," is simply showing her lack of control. The strong-willed child knows immediately upon hearing the idle threat that he has the upper hand. No mother is capable of enforcing the threat to ground her child for life (and maybe not even for a month), and indeed, the parent also would be grounded. Believe it or not, I hear fathers threaten, "I'll break your arm if you do that." Or, "I'll knock you to the other side of tomorrow if you don't stop." These unattractive, highly offensive statements are not credible and result in the strong-willed child winning the battle. The unreasonable threats made by a loving (though unthinking) parent will never be carried out.

"We were at my sister's house having dinner, and she was trying to get her little boy to stay in his seat. He wanted

to get down and play with my two-year-old. He did not
want to finish his dinner. Finally, she let him know that
he was not trapped at the table forever. She simply stated,
'You can get down and play once all of that food is off
your plate.' At that point, she continued eating until
Brian announced, 'Mom, I can get down now.' All the
food was off his plate and placed on the table."

Being clear about your instructions is as important as being clear
about the consequences. In the early stages of the journey it is not too
early to discipline your child. Undoubtedly the form that discipline
takes will vary as the child matures.

"For three days I tried to get my three-year-old to clean
the toy room. Each time, she would very calmly tell me
'no' and walk away. Finally, Halloween rolled around,
and we were talking about trick-or-treating. I told her,
'If you want to go trick-or-treating, you have to clean
the toy room.' And she said she didn't want to. I said,
'Sarah, if you don't do your job, you are not going trick-
or-treating.' She didn't want to cooperate, so I let twenty
minutes go by, and then I sat her down. I explained very
calmly: 'Your sisters are going to get their costumes on,
and Daddy's going to take them outside, and they are
going to run around and yell "trick-or—treat" and get
lots of candy.'

She nonchalantly said, 'I already have candy,' and
walked out of the room. A couple of hours later it was
almost time to go, and the older kids decided to put on
their costumes. I was getting their makeup done, and
Sarah came running in reporting, 'I want to pick up the
toys. I want to go, too.'

'No, it's too late,' I said. 'It's time to get the costumes on.'

So she walked out of the room, and fifteen minutes later she walked back in. 'I cleaned the whole toy room by myself.'

That is what I wanted her to do for three days, so I helped her get into her costume and let her trick-or-treat. Mistakenly, I thought I won the battle. And then I realized that my three-year-old won, because she did exactly what she wanted to do when she wanted to do it and not when I asked her to do it. I actually lost the battle."

Blessed is the man you discipline, O Lord,
the man you teach from your law;
you grant him relief from days of trouble.
PSALM 94:12–13

So how do you discipline a strong-willed child? There are many different ways. A parent can give the child an explanation or a "time-out." These are sometimes quite effective. So is spanking. We did not use only one form of discipline with our strong-willed child or with our other children. The most important thing to remember is that discipline must NEVER be administered in anger. Spanking is a form of discipline that does not require a long time frame to accomplish. Someone asked me once if I typically used a time-out with my strong-willed child. No, I didn't. As I reflected on Aaron's strong-willed nature, I realized that if I had, he would probably *still* be in time-out and would not have been able to attend college. No, we had a paddle, "Mr. Sore Butt." I know, it's not a very elegant title, and I'm sure my mother would have preferred the name "Mr. Sore Bottom." Nevertheless, it was effective.

Punishment is meant to deter negative behavior, that is, to dissuade and discourage inappropriate or potentially dangerous behavior and defiance. Your punishment must have impact. A light tap on the bottom of a diapered strong-willed toddler is not accomplishing your goal of punishment.

It has been over two decades since I taught school, and many things have changed in the classroom and the nation since that time. But I still remember the day that a student named Joseph stepped over the line in my class, and I escorted him to the principal's office. We decided that Joseph's behavior warranted a spanking, and with the principal's approval and watchful eye, I administered one swift swat to Joseph's bottom. He went back to the room, and I followed at a much closer distance than he realized. I entered the room just as Joseph was bragging that it "didn't hurt at all!"

"No problem," I said, "we can take care of that." And back we went to the office. I swatted harder the second time. My initial punishment was not sufficient to deter poor behavior. If you do not see a change in behavior when your punishment is administered, it could be because you did not use adequate force.

"My niece, Melissa, was in kindergarten for two months when her parents got a call from the teacher. 'I don't know what to do with Melissa,' lamented the instructor. 'Every day when it is time to pick up the toys, she refuses to help.'

Melissa's dad promised to try and get to the bottom of the problem. That day when she came home from school, he confronted her about not picking up the toys at school. Her reply was simple, honest, and straightforward. 'Look, Dad,' she said, 'all the teacher does is make you sit in the corner in time-out if you don't help pick up the toys. I'd rather sit in a chair than have to pick up all those toys. So, I just make sure that she sees me not picking up the toys, and pretty soon she sits me on the chair. I get to watch all the other kids pick up the toys and it's over.'"

The previous story is an obvious example of the attempted deterrent failing miserably. Melissa preferred punishment to losing control and having to perform an unpleasant task—in this case, it was picking up toys.

> *Simply let your "Yes" be "Yes," and your "No," "No";*
> *anything beyond this comes from the evil one.*
> MATTHEW 5:37

What about the parent who sets the boundaries, witnesses her child cross them, follows through on the predetermined discipline, and then begins to feel sorry for her child, and cancels the punishment in midstream, before the entire "sentence" is served? Woe to that parent. The fancy term for what transpired is intermittent reinforcement. Modern science has proved that sporadically reinforced behavior is very difficult to extinguish.

Parents exercise intermittent reinforcement for two main reasons. They feel sorry for their child. (After all, Little Johnny has been inside for two whole days now, and all the neighborhood kids are frolicking right outside his window.) Or, they are too exhausted to administer the punishment. Strong-willed children are persistent, and as the parent of one, it is important for you to be *more* persistent. If your strong-willed child can wear you down or convince you that you were overboard with your discipline, he will. If you are inconsistent with your discipline, your strong-willed child will battle longer, imagining that this is another time that you will give in. If you are consistent, the chances of your strong-willed child eventually giving up the fight are increased.

"I have a very strong-willed child. She is so difficult that it's been putting a wedge between my husband and me, especially at bedtime. We're having difficulty finding time alone together, because she doesn't want to go to sleep at night. She says she is scared. She starts cracking her knuckles and licking her lips. She doesn't want to sleep alone. We are asked why Mommy and Daddy get

to sleep in the same bed, and she can't sleep in the bed
with us. A lot of times we end up giving in because we're
so tired, and we just want to go to sleep. All of our alone
time is gone, and it's really causing friction in our rela-
tionship. HELP!!!"

Giving in is the opposite of winning the battle. It is losing the battle. Remember that winning the battle is one of the "Rules of the Road"
for a successful journey. I was most guilty in this department when it
came to potty training. Again, there was a stark contrast between my
first, compliant child, and my second, strong-willed child.

I can still hear my mother saying, "All you have to do is feed him
oatmeal for breakfast, every day at the same time, and then have him sit
on the potty." It sounds so simple, doesn't it? And that is exactly what I
did with Matthew, and within weeks he was done having accidents. (Do
I need to remind you again of my amazing skills as a mother? Just wait,
my big head will deflate soon enough.) So what did I do with Aaron?
Why, of course, I did the same thing. And when he didn't respond as
rapidly as his older brother, I immediately tried plan B. That was the
reward plan, as I recall. And in a few days when that had no obvious
result, I went to plan C. I think that one was some kind of a point system. By plan F, I was thoroughly frustrated with Aaron and with potty
training. Talk about something that he alone was able to control. In retrospect, I realize that I was not consistent or persistent. I intermittently
reinforced his noncompliance by switching strategies. In short, I didn't
do a very good job. Fortunately, he finally decided that it was in his best
interest to join the ranks of the potty trained.

Bowel and bladder control (how glamorous) are very difficult for
the parent of a strong-willed child to control. The best plan is to convince your child that he wants to acquiesce and control these functions
as the adult population does. And whatever your method, stick to it.

Parents, every day you have to decide where you'll draw the line—
what behavior is permissible and what will not be tolerated. You'll have
to be ready for battle every day until your child makes his own decision
to stop battling. The hope is that his determination for control will
lessen each day. But until he decides to acquiesce, I guarantee you that

you will be pushed and tested. The more often you give in, the worse it will get, and the longer the process will take. If you hold firm, your strong-willed child will eventually give up engaging in many of the fights. Don't be shortsighted. Raising a strong-willed child is not a sprint; it's a marathon.

A Closer Look with Aaron

Mom told you the story of Dad and me "eyeball-to-eyeball" on the stairs. And she wondered out loud if I actually believed Dad when he said that I had to obey him. It wasn't really a question of whether or not Dad was telling the truth. That wasn't the issue. The issue was whether or not I wanted to suffer the consequences of disobeying him. My Dad was always fair and never administered punishment in anger, but when you were spanked for disobeying, you knew you were spanked.

Some parents find that discussing an issue with their children is an effective way to discipline them. My guess is that if that system works, the child is not actually strong-willed. As an adult, I recently saw a television show about disciplining children. One mother told the story of her three-year-old not wanting to stay in his bed at night unless she was in his room. Her solution? She pulled a rocker into the room and told her son that she would sit and read while he fell asleep, but if he got out of bed, she would have to leave the room and shut the door. Interestingly, her plan worked after a week. At first, she had to stand up from her chair when he hopped out of bed. But after she threatened to leave the room, he went back to his bed. She reported that soon he was staying in bed and falling asleep right away.

As I listened to this mother giving her discipline advice, I realized that gaining control over that situation would have been no problem for me (or any strong-willed child). I would simply get out of bed and force the mother to leave the room. Then, after she shut the door, I would scream bloody murder.

At that point, the mother would have an obvious dilemma. Because no one was in the room to stop me, no one to physically put a hand over my mouth, the odds are she would feel compelled to check to be sure I was all right and try to calm and silence me. And as soon as she reentered the room, I would immediately jump into bed. Then if she had decided to spank me, she'd feel guilty because I was back in bed, right where I was supposed to be. If I got out of bed again and she left, I'd simply repeat the scenario. The probability of this woman's plan working with a strong-willed child was, in my estimation, not very high. A strong-willed child is capable of almost immeasurable persistence, unless he is ultimately convinced that the discipline is too uncomfortable.

What is difficult for most people to understand is the motivation of a strong-willed child. The strong-willed child will choose the stated punishment in order to be in control, especially if the child considers the punishment moderate. Too many times the parent is shortsighted. A strong-willed child may choose to miss a party, not get dessert, or be sent to his room, because those things are really no big deal. A guilt-ridden parent (this is false guilt induced by the strong-willed child) is not likely to choose to fight that particular battle again. The child is now running the show. The strong-willed child has chosen a small sacrifice for a big payoff. And usually, the parent has no clue. "Why didn't he want to go outside? All I asked him to do was pick up his toys. Doesn't this child ever give in? I hate seeing him missing out on all the fun." If a strong-willed child can make his parent feel guilty for carrying out the punishment, he may have lost a skirmish, but he has advanced in winning the war. What is the key for the parent? Keep things in perspective. Always look at the big picture.

And, if and when you leave the room to gain your composure, go ahead and get your blood pressure down and calm yourself, but don't ever change the edict you made prior to your exit. Don't change the rules. Think before you make them. Be fair and stick to your decision.

You probably also need to know that, even after the punishment has been administered, it's really not over. I remember getting paddled and screaming like crazy. The punishment definitely hurt, but the screaming was totally to get Mom's sympathy. I would respond to reasonable and adequate spanking like someone was ripping my leg out of the socket. I tried to convince the folks that I was going to be permanently injured. And Dad (the guy who'd "been there and done that") would say, "You have three minutes to cry until I spank you again." That was smart and effective. If he hadn't said that, I would have continued the manipulation indefinitely.

Mom's suggestion that discipline ought to never be administered in anger is a good one. But I want you to think about a more radical possibility. We've all heard the cliché "This is going to hurt me more than it hurts you." Some of you have probably said it. That statement implies that the parent enforcing the discipline will be experiencing some degree of pain, which is probably true to some extent. Now, here's my idea. What if an attempt was made to discipline with no emotion whatsoever? We all know that it is wrong to discipline in anger. I'm suggesting that neither disciplining in sympathy nor frustration nor pity nor commiseration is the optimal condition. My dad was able to accomplish nonemotional punishment the great majority of the time (as opposed to my mother). He dispensed the predetermined punishment as a sales clerk might hand you a product you purchased. You selected the item, paid for it, and now it was yours. The sales clerk has little emotion (positive or negative). She is giving you what you have chosen and deserve. In the same way, a parent giving a strong-willed child what he has chosen and deserves should try to do it without emotion. The truthful message to your child should be "This is going to hurt *you* more than it hurts me." That doesn't indicate lack of love or caring; it is merely healthy detachment in delivering punishment.

A Good Word from John, the Resident Dad

There are many ideas about how and why the discipline detour has been created. One young dad suggested that the parents of today had "bought into the lie that the opposite of love was discipline." He went on to say that it *had* to be a lie because we know from God's Word that "the Lord disciplines those he loves, as a father the son he delights in" (Proverbs 3:12); and "because the Lord disciplines those he loves, and he punishes everyone he accepts as a son" (Hebrews 12:6).

With our heavenly Father as our example, we are required to do the same—to discipline those we love. Loving your child and building a strong and positive relationship occurs long before you are required as a parent to discipline your child. Your loving relationship develops before you ever have to set boundaries and deliver consequences. And the love continues throughout your child's lifetime.

The purpose of discipline is to change your child's behavior when it is dangerous, destructive, or defiant. Discipline is an extension of love. I loved our sons from the day they were born. That is when love begins—maybe even sooner. Being diligent in the task of discipline is easier when you realize that it is a display of your love. Loving discipline is modeled by our heavenly Father and is a necessary part of being a parent.

When it comes to the strong-willed child there is one more element that can cause a parent to take the discipline detour. Strong-willed children are very persistent and very determined to be in control of their world. They can outlast a parent who is unaware of those two things. As of this moment, you are not one of those uninformed parents. You will most likely have to be stern ("no emotion") and firm in your discipline with a strong-willed child. Remember, you must win the battle you have wisely chosen to fight. It will not necessarily be a pleasant task, but always remember that your motivation is love and that your desire is to guide your child into responsible adulthood. When you enforce the boundaries you have set for your child, you are not the "bad cop." In many ways you are the "good cop," helping your child learn to temper his strong-willed nature and use it in an appropriate way.

Help your strong-willed child temper his nature to glorify God.

CHAPTER THREE

The Journey Continues: Kindergarten to Grade Six

Give, and it will be given to you.
A good measure, pressed down,
shaken together and running over,
will be poured into your lap.
For with the measure you use,
it will be measured to you.

LUKE 6:38

The verse above is one example of a paradox found in God's Word. The Bible contains numerous paradoxes. When we give, we receive. We die to live (Matthew 10:39, Philippians 1:21). Many who are first will be last, and the last first (Mark 10:31). These seemingly contradictory statements can be confusing, like the paradoxes in the life of a strong-willed child. For example, the strong-willed child wants to control himself and yet wants to be controlled by his loving parents and other responsible adults. That apparently inconsistent attitude is manifest in the life of a strong-willed child. He wants to live in the presence and structure of just and fair rules.

As Aaron's parents, it was our hope that his desire to control his world would be lovingly overruled by his teachers. We looked forward to his teachers being caring enough to make him mind authority. We hoped that they would respect and appreciate his creative, out-of-the-box thinking and his enthusiasm for life. In the grade school years, Aaron intersected with many adults who encouraged him and some adults who were very discouraging.

In grade school, Aaron was often disappointed by lack of fairness in the classroom. The reasoning of a strong-willed child is more black-and-white than that of other children. They trust that when rules are made, they will not be changed. They are intolerant of behavior that is not perceived as just.

"Life is not fair. God is good. And this too shall pass."[1]

SHIRLEY DAHLQUIST

One Monday, a primary school teacher of Aaron's declared that "Button Day" was on Friday, and instructed the children to wear as many pins and buttons as they could find. There was to be a prize awarded for the most buttons. Aaron took this challenge seriously. He raided my desk and found campaign and advertising buttons, and he decked himself out from head to toe. Upon arriving at school that day, proudly displaying what was undoubtedly the winning button collection, his teacher told him that he had to give some of his buttons away to the students who had forgotten about the assignment. What? Before the judging? Certainly that couldn't be fair! Tears flowed as his teacher forced him to give up pieces of his blue-ribbon button collection. She expected him to unselfishly share his buttons and to do it in a good-natured manner, even though this was a total change in the rules for the day. Aaron would not have minded sharing his buttons if that was the plan from the beginning. If the explanation of "Button Day" was to collect and distribute buttons, he would have been more than happy to be the chief button provider.

Aaron couldn't understand why his teacher was changing the rules in the middle of the game. He expected her to understand that he had searched long and hard for this collection of buttons. She never indicated that he was in charge of bringing extra buttons for the less motivated or more forgetful students in the class. She forced him to give up his buttons, and he did as he was told but not before his feelings were hurt. That didn't seem to matter to his teacher.

The unfair order of Aaron's teacher wounded him. And, unfortunately, that set the stage for the rest of the year with this particular teacher. She did not like Aaron. Perhaps she didn't before the infamous button incident but definitely not after it. She perceived him as selfish and didn't like his questioning her rule change. At one parent-teacher meeting, she informed us that Aaron was merely "an average child with no great potential." We should not expect anything more than that. As someone who expects the best in people and in situations, this thought was not only foreign to me but also distasteful. An adult who changes the rules and makes the strong-willed child pay for the change is, if not a roadblock on the journey, at least a great big speed bump!

Another of Aaron's elementary school teachers had a totally different approach. Rather than declare him to be something less than he was, she specifically asked us how we thought she could best help Aaron develop his potential. We encouraged this teacher to hold a tough line with him, not let him dictate, and make him abide by the rules she established. Delightfully, she followed our suggestions, and Aaron's experience with her was very positive. This teacher was wise and mature, and Aaron reaped the benefit of her wisdom. As the parent of a strong-willed child, you can offer understanding and insights that can assist a teacher in helping your child.

> *"There is something very powerful about . . . someone believing in you, someone giving you another chance."*[2]
> SHEILA WALSH

> *Therefore I do not run like a man running aimlessly;*
> *I do not fight like a man beating the air.*
> 1 CORINTHIANS 9:26

In second grade Aaron and I had a battle that is permanently etched in both of our memories. He was in the top reading group at school, and the students were given an assignment to write a creative poem for an area-wide competition. The problem with it, as Aaron saw it, was that it was not for a grade in class. They were writing this poem to be entered in a contest. Aaron didn't see any use in that! What a silly waste of time. He didn't want to enter a contest.

Thankfully, he didn't express these feelings to his reading teacher. Instead he announced to me on the evening before the due date, that he was NOT going to do the "stupid" assignment. Of course, I told him differently. It was a battle that I was going to fight and win. Aaron was fired up for the conflict, and it was one of the most intense battles of the will we ever fought. At one point, I literally pinned him in the chair, almost sat on his lap and informed him, "I will not create this poem for you. *You* are going to do it. I have a piece of paper, and I will take down dictation as you compose the poem." (How many times is a stenographer that forceful?) We sat there as he protested loudly. I did not give an inch, literally, and finally he started shouting out ideas for the poem.

Ultimately his creative work evolved into this: "Busy bear, busy bear, don't bother me! I have work of my own—like gathering honey and other nutty things. So, DON'T BOTHER ME!" Years later, we laughed at his finished product. There was no doubt that he was trying to tell me not to bother him. Fortunately, I didn't read between the lines that evening. I was just so glad he had actually produced something to hand in to his teacher for the contest. I was exhausted from the battle, but it was one worth fighting.

By the way, "Busy Bear" won second place in the three-county contest. Aaron received a certificate and savings bond at a ceremony held at the junior college. And he thoroughly enjoyed the accolades. "Busy Bear" was an important victory, and it was one battle that I fought without the aid of my husband, John. Usually he was there to lead the charge, but he was gone on assignment with the Air Force Reserve, and this was one of those times when *I* was flying solo.

Years later I discovered a biographical form that Aaron completed in the third grade. Among the many sentences that the students were asked to complete were these:

"Something that I am afraid of is _____." Aaron drew scribbles through that line. In his mind there was NOTHING he was afraid of.

Then came the next line:

"Something that I am NOT afraid of is _____." In that blank he had boldly written "Mom." I shall be forever thankful that I was not alone raising my strong-willed child.

There was one year in grade school that was especially unpleasant for Aaron. Amazingly, John and I didn't even realize what was transpiring until the day we got *the phone call* with only six weeks left in the school year. "Could you please come in for an appointment?" was the request. "I've been having a little trouble with Aaron."

"A little trouble" did not prepare us for what we heard later that day. As John and I sat down with the teacher, she told us about Aaron's behavior in the classroom. She gave the class an assignment that Aaron decided not to do. The class was to write in their journals every day. "That's silly," he declared. So what did he do? He organized a coup d'état, and most of the class boycotted the assignment. (Remember, I told you that a strong-willed child could be charming and persuasive!) We didn't know anything about this incident or his rebellion until we met with the teacher that day.

"Every experience
God gives us, Every person
he puts in our lives,
Is the perfect preparation
for the future
That only he can see."[3]
BETH MOORE

Was I embarrassed? Yes! Was I disappointed in Aaron's poor choice? Yes! Was I amazed that this teacher had let the conflict get to this point? Yes! She was unable to control this elementary school boy. He was allowed to take control, and now in tears, she was meeting with us, his parents. "What should I do?" she wanted to know.

Even though part of me wanted to scold the teacher for relinquishing her power to Aaron, we knew that it was in Aaron's best interest for us to take control of the situation. We told her that she would have no more trouble with Aaron and that he would write in his journal as instructed. (This guarantee was a little easier to make because there were only a few weeks left in the school year.)

That evening we made it very clear to Aaron that he could no longer behave poorly in class, and if he did, he would pay the price at home. He believed us, but he was not happy. My recollection is that every single day of school, for the rest of the year, he cried before the bus arrived. (And I cried after the bus drove away.) The teacher wanted to win the battle, but her authority had been so undermined throughout the year that she could not. We came to her rescue, though Aaron felt that he needed rescuing, too. Yet, forcing him to give up control was definitely in his best interest.

A Closer Look with Aaron

I can't believe that the teacher *only* told Mom and Dad about the journal boycott. That was not the first incident. I guess it was the straw that broke the camel's back. And I know why it did. The majority of the class decided to "get on board" with my refusal to complete the daily assignment. And because of that, our teacher couldn't use the fear of poor grades as motivation. If she did, most of the kids in the class would have received an F on the assignment. Can you imagine explaining the failing grade to someone's parents? "Your child flunked this assignment, because I couldn't convince her to do it." Now *that* sounds professional. So she finally had to call in the big guns. She told my parents about the problem at hand—but believe me—she lost control long before that.

The problems began about four or five weeks into the school year. We were in a science unit studying solids, liquids, and gases. She gave us the following definitions for each: A solid is something that holds its own shape and has a constant volume. A liquid takes the shape of the container and has a constant volume. A gas takes the shape of the container and has a variable volume. Simple enough, right? (Can you believe that I can still remember these?)

Well, I got to thinking, what is ice cream? Is it a solid or a liquid? So I raised my hand and asked, "What is ice cream? When you scoop it out, it takes the shape of the ice cream scoop like a liquid. But when you put it from the scoop into the bowl, it holds that shape and doesn't take the shape of the bowl."

I was not trying to be a smart aleck when I asked that question. It just fascinated me. My teacher, however, was not fascinated. She did not know the answer, did not care about the answer, and was completely annoyed that I asked the question. Her reply was something like, "It doesn't make any difference." What kind of answer is that? I raised my hand again, and when she acknowledged me I simply said, "You don't know, do you?" That completely flustered her, and she ignored me and moved rapidly through the lesson.

The ice cream question was the beginning of the end for that teacher. I didn't care at all that she didn't know the answer. I didn't know the answer either. If I did know, I wouldn't have asked. But it was a good question, an interesting one, and she wouldn't admit that it was one we'd have to research. She was not equipped to deal with a grade school kid who could ask a question that she couldn't answer. From that point forward, she was a target for me. I looked for opportunities to frustrate her, wondering if she would ever take charge.

I could tell you story after story. (Sorry, Mom.) For example, we had to write sentences with our spelling words, and we were told to put the punctuation at the end of the sentence. I did—*way at the end*—as close to the right-hand margin as I could get, regardless of the length of the sentence. She'd mark all my sentences wrong, but she could not give me a poor grade, since I (technically) followed her directions.

We had a rule—no gum, water, soda, etc., during the day —only milk during milk break. That was the rule, although she chose to drink coffee and soda all day long. So one day I saved my milk and brought it out much later to sip as I was reading my history lesson. "Aaron, milk time is over. There are no drinks in class," was her reaction. And my reply? "You have your coffee, and I have my milk. If there are no drinks in class, then why do you get to have one?" She informed me that the rule only applied to students, not to teachers. Since I decided that the rule was unfair, and I knew that she was vulnerable, I chose to make an issue of it. My battleground wasn't the classroom. Instead I took my protest to the playground. While we waited in line to play four-square or to swing, I'd say to one of my classmates, "Can you believe that our teacher gets to drink in class? That's not fair." It didn't take much to get the majority of the class inflamed over the injustice of the rule. Before long, every drink of coffee or pop she took was met with one of my contemporaries saying, "No drinks in class."

The pressure became too great for her. Rather than control the students in her class and insist they stop their new aggravating habit, she put a little table out in the hall. And that was where she left her coffee and soda when she entered the room. Then when she wanted a sip, she stepped outside. Evidently, she felt guilty about drinking in the classroom. Her giving in to our pressure diminished our respect even more. And it liberated the kids in the class. Slowly but surely, she was disintegrating in front of us. She lost the respect of the majority of the students in the class. And she seemed to be helpless when it came to reestablishing her rightful control. After all, what was she going to do? Call in the principal or phone our parents and tell them that we had forced her to drink her coffee in the hall? She was obviously embarrassed and wanted to keep the uprising confidential.

I didn't enter school that fall with the idea of making her life miserable. And she probably didn't imagine that she could be challenged so severely. The hole in the dam occurred when I realized her unwillingness to admit that she didn't know something. I didn't expect her to know everything, but I did expect her to be truthful and honest about what she did not know. Her immaturity triggered my strong-willed nature, and I took control.

After the meeting with my parents, she knew that I was going to have to tow the mark. She finally had leverage. Unfortunately, by this time she had an understandable personal vendetta against me. She was so angry at this point that she wanted revenge. And she was able to achieve it to some degree.

There was a student in our classroom who had many serious problems. Years later, in fact, he was imprisoned, and he has not, up to this point, been a contributing member of society. The possibility of a bleak future was evident even in the grade school years. One of his antisocial behaviors was spitting on his classmates. Whenever he behaved in this manner, the teacher disciplined him until one day when he haphazardly spit on me. "Aaron spit on me first," was the defense of this young man. "No, I didn't," was my reply, backed by several unsolicited testimonies from my classmates. "Well," responded the teacher. "I wasn't there to see it, so I can't be sure who was at fault." Touché! The spitter walked away with no punishment, noted who was the "free target," and I spent the remainder of the school year dodging the vengeance of the teacher in the form of an out-of-control classmate. I knew I couldn't strike back, because she would never come to my defense. It didn't matter if I was innocent or not. In her mind I was guilty. It was a painful last few weeks of school.

A Good Word from John, the Resident Dad

Your strong-willed child has many things to learn during the elementary school years and it will be your responsibility to help with the learning process. Strong-willed children must be taught to develop long-term thinking. In school they may win a battle with a teacher but go on to lose the war. Help them realize that some battles should never be fought, especially ones with teachers or others in authority.

Another challenge for a strong-willed child is the concept that life is not fair. You have already read about one of Aaron's first introductions to that. It came when he was instructed to give up the buttons he had diligently gathered in order to win the contest. Although the change of rules was not fair, it was reality.

Finally, it is important for you to look for ways to reinforce the positive attributes your son or daughter possesses simply because of their strong-willed nature. We had just such an opportunity as Aaron's journey continued into elementary school.

Aaron was a member of an after-school soccer team. He really enjoyed the sport. It gave him the opportunity to run and play with other kids and also gave him a feeling of accomplishment because he was able to do well in the competition. One day something happened that changed his feelings about the activity. For whatever reason, the volunteer coach became very annoyed with the entire team. His annoyance turned into anger and his anger was manifested in very foul language. At one point he yelled at the entire group of boys and referred to them in terms that, in my opinion, should not be used by civilized people.

Aaron was quite offended, and in protest, walked off the practice field. When the coach came over to confront him, Aaron simply said that soccer was supposed to be fun and it wasn't fun when the coach used bad language to scold the team. Aaron's straightforward response surprised and probably infuriated the coach. His reply was "Fine. Then go home!" "I will," said Aaron, "as soon as my ride gets here."

Aaron was very sad because what had been fun was turning out to be not so fun. Days later the coach called our home to apologize and to ask Aaron to return to the team. Although the apology was accepted, Aaron chose to forgo playing soccer. Perhaps he doubted whether the apology was genuine. Who knows . . . but taking a stand against coarse language was to be applauded! He was right. The coach should not have spoken to those young boys (or to anyone else for that matter) using foul language. We supported Aaron's decision and let him know that we realized the decision was difficult and also was correct.

Your strong-willed child will amaze you with his willingness to take a stand for what is right if you have helped him understand what is truly right . . . what God says about right and wrong.

You are your child's teacher even after they enter school and encounter other teachers.

That was an awful year for Aaron! In our school district, the policy used to be that parents could request a specific teacher for the coming year. I went into the principal's office weeks after our meeting with

Aaron's teacher and simply said, "I don't know who would be the best teacher for Aaron. I need your help. Please suggest someone who will love him." And she did.

The next year was a time of healing for our strong-willed son. His subsequent teacher did love him. She appreciated his out-of-the-box thinking and encouraged him to solve problems that were not necessarily in her lesson plans. If Aaron asked a question in class about something only vaguely related to the discussion, she would reply, "That's a great question, Aaron. I'm not sure what the answer is, but maybe you can look it up in the encyclopedia during break and find something." Her reaction could have been, "Aaron, we are NOT discussing that right now. Please do not waste my time with your unrelated questions." To a strong-willed child, an answer like that is internally translated: "I don't know the answer, and I'm not going to admit it, because I'm trying to convince everyone that I know everything." And with that answer, a strong-willed child has discovered a chink in the armor—an adult who is not willing to admit that he or she doesn't know everything—an insecure, immature, and vulnerable adult.

"We should be in the business of building people up. There are too many people in the demolition business today."[4]
NORMAN VINCENT PEALE

His new teacher was not threatened by his questions. She was not a pushover; she was simply respectful of him. And he returned the respect. At one point in the year, the class bully lashed out at the teacher, and she had to physically restrain him—at least she tried. As she literally wrestled with his arms and upper body, Aaron came to her rescue and grabbed the bully's legs, preventing the child from continuing to kick their teacher. Aaron could not bear the thought of someone hurting this kind person. He risked his well-being (and becoming a later target of this bully) as an act of loyalty to someone he loved and respected. What a change in behavior, a logical response to his new teacher's behavior.

*Everyone must submit himself to the governing authorities,
for there is no authority except that which God has established.*
ROMANS 13:1

In the years of kindergarten through grade six, Aaron's life intersected with more positive, encouraging adults than discouraging ones. He encountered more than one wonderful teacher who demanded and deserved his respect. One of those came in the later years of elementary school. The defining battle with this teacher came almost immediately upon introduction. Aaron was testing to see what *this* school year would bring. His teacher pronounced a word differently than Aaron had heard it pronounced, so he chose to correct her. When she disagreed, he jumped up from his seat, got a dictionary, and started to look up the word. His teacher marched over to Aaron, shut the dictionary with force, and loudly slammed it on his desk. Then she told him to go outside the room. In a few minutes, she joined him in the hall, handed him a piece of paper and a pencil, and told him that he would not speak to her that way. Furthermore, he was to write her an apology.

> *"The man incapable of making a mistake is incapable of anything."*
> ABRAHAM LINCOLN

Stunned and a little surprised, he wrote that apology and took it in to her. She read it and responded to Aaron, "I forgive you," and that was the end of it. She immediately buried the hatchet. She was mature. She was secure. She demanded and deserved Aaron's respect. Not only did he give it to her, he loved being in her classroom that year. He felt safe, comfortable, and respected. He knew where the boundaries were placed and that they would be enforced in no uncertain terms.

Aaron treated both of these excellent teachers with the utmost respect. Their personalities and methods of teaching and interacting with their students were not identical. However, these women were mature and confident and appreciated the finer points of a strong-willed child. They were very positive influences in Aaron's life. Remember, one of the paradoxes of a strong-willed child is that this child who desires control of his world also desires to be lovingly controlled. More paradoxes to come. Next, we will examine what people assume about the strong-willed child versus what is actually true.

> *Not many of you should presume to be teachers, my brothers,*
> *because you know that we who teach will be judged more strictly.*
> JAMES 3:1

CHAPTER FOUR

Assumptions vs. Actualities

*Now we see but a poor reflection as in a
mirror; then we shall see face to face.
Now I know in part; then I shall know
fully, even as I am fully known.*
1 CORINTHIANS 13:12

People make many assumptions in regard to strong-willed children. Once accepted, assumptions that are false can impede the progress of the strong-willed child on his way to competent, confident adulthood. If you are operating under any of these kinds of assumptions, you and your strong-willed child are bound to run into roadblocks on the journey.

There is little research available on this topic of strong-willed children. Perhaps it is because it is difficult to qualify and quantify their behavior. In the absence of extensive scientific study, I have conducted my own informal research. Obviously, I have personal experiences to draw from, and I have spoken to and heard from thousands of parents who identify one or more of their children as strong-willed. This personal analysis has led to the debunking of several assumptions that can impede the progress of a strong-willed child on his lifetime journey.

Assumption vs. Actuality #1
Tough vs. Tender

*Consider the ravens: They do not sow or reap,
they have no storeroom or barn;*

yet God feeds them. And how much more valuable
you are than birds!
LUKE 12:24

It is often assumed that the strong-willed child is as tough as nails and that he has no problem with being mistreated or ridiculed. This is an untrue assumption that often results from the strong opinions and in-your-face behavior of a strong-willed child. It is a misconception that a strong-willed child is insensitive. Because they consistently question authority and are willing to choose punishment over compliance, it is assumed that they are unfeeling. A strong-willed child appears to push his way through all situations, yet if one looks closely, he wears his heart on his sleeve. The truth of the matter is that strong-willed children are very compassionate. Although they are typically the last to "give in," they are often the first to feel compassion for another and offer comfort.

The strong-willed child, like everyone else, has the desire to be loved, appreciated, and treated with respect. But because their responses tend to be so abrupt, people assume that they want that same sort of abruptness in return. Because of the way these children are wired, others do not perceive them as capable of or interested in tenderness. But a strong-willed child can be hurt just like any other child and is often mis-read because of his strong responses. An adult who does not encourage the strengths of a strong-willed child, deeming him tough and more welcoming of criticism than another child, is an adult who may create a serious roadblock in the journey of a strong-willed child.

God is our refuge and strength,
an ever-present help in trouble.
PSALM 46:1

As the parent of a strong-willed child, it is important for you to pro-vide a safe environment where your child is encouraged, corrected, and supported. You may have to be his advocate in situations beyond the home. When I say this, I don't mean that you unequivocally take the position of your strong-willed child and defend behavior that should not be defended. Remember, we did not support Aaron's coup in grade school. We did, however, sympathize with him when an earlier teacher unfairly changed the rules on "Button Day." When you are your child's advocate, you are doing what is in his best interest. It is NEVER in your child's best interest to condone improper behavior or poor choices. Remembering that your strong-willed child has tender emotions that are often vulnerable will keep *your* heart tender toward him and keep him moving forward.

Look for opportunities to encourage your child. God's Word is filled with reminders and instructions to encourage. One of my favorites is "Therefore encourage one another and build each other up, just as in fact you are doing" (1 Thessalonians 5:11). God's Word is encouraging encouragement, and it is applauding the encouragers, too. Catch your strong-willed child in the act of doing something right, and then encourage him to keep it up.

First Thessalonians 2:11–12 is another verse that can apply to the parenting of a strong-willed child: "For you know that we dealt with each of you as a father deals with his own children, encouraging, comforting and urging you to live lives worthy of God, who calls you into his kingdom and glory." It is your privilege and responsibility to provide encouragement to your tenderhearted, strong-willed child. Don't let his rough exterior fool you. As an adult, Aaron has commented on the powerful effect of being raised with a "You can do it!" attitude. That message was so ingrained that it was an unquestioned assurance in his life. It fostered confidence and made pretentiousness and arrogance unnecessary.

Assumption vs. Actuality #2
Discipline Doesn't Work vs.
Increased Demand for Loving Discipline

Train a child in the way he should go,
and when he is old he will not turn from it.
PROVERBS 22:6

Wait! Didn't we already have a whole chapter on discipline? Yes, and at the risk of repeating some of the same principles, we are going to tackle the topic once again. Discipline is one of the more difficult components of raising a strong-willed child.

Let's begin with a simple premise that we haven't covered yet. *Why* do we discipline our children? We discipline them to teach them to obey. This is important for a number of reasons. Children are unaware of the dangers of the world. Teaching a preschool child to not go out in the street or to hold your hand in the parking lot is an act of love. Teaching your grade school child to not accept a ride with a stranger or to be discreet when supplying information to a caller is important for his well-being. We make our children mind in order to keep them safe.

I was traveling recently and encountered a situation where discipline was definitely lacking. I was at Chicago O'Hare airport, one of the busiest airports in the world, and I was moving toward the baggage carousel to wait for the arrival of my luggage. The previous flight was very full, and there was a large crowd gathering as the bags began to move around the conveyor. In front of me was a young mother with two children in a double stroller. One was a baby and the other was a boy probably about three years old. As I observed this family, I saw the boy squirming in his seat and heard his mother say, "Sit down, please. Daddy will be right back. You can't get out in this crowd."

The little boy completely ignored his mother and actually seemed to pursue his escape with even more fervor. In a matter of seconds, he was entirely reversed in his seat, standing up, and preparing to bail out of the stroller. "SIT DOWN! You cannot get out of there!!" said his mother sternly.

I wanted to say, "Oh yes he can. Look at him." And before I could even finish my thought, he was out and racing toward the baggage carousel. I lost sight of him almost immediately and imagine that his mother did, too. I'm assuming that somewhere between his point of escape and the Tri-State Tollway, his father intercepted him. His mother could not control him enough to keep him from potential harm. I'm sure I was openmouthed for more than a few seconds as I pondered the possible negative outcome of this young man's breakout. This independent, potentially danger-prone youngster was in charge, and I am willing to guess that his mother was in for big trouble.

Obey your leaders and submit to their authority.
They keep watch over you as men who must give an account.
HEBREWS 13:17

Disciplining our children is not only for their safety. We also discipline them to teach them respect for others and for property. Jumping on Grandma's couch may not harm the child, but it is not respectful to Grandma or to her property. Teaching our children to respect others helps them to develop into responsible adults, able to interact in our society. I read an issue of the *Ladies' Home Journal* that contained an article entitled "The Perils of the Pushover Parent." Not only was this article soundly supporting the necessity of discipline, but it said that "parents who chronically cave in to their kids' whims are actually doing them harm."[1] Continuing on, it read:

> *Kids may relish their grasp on power, but child-rearing experts from across the political spectrum agree that it can be hazardous to their long-term emotional health. "Kids absolutely need structure and limits," says Laurence Steinberg, Ph.D., a psychology professor at Temple University, in Philadelphia, and author of* You *and* Your Adolescent. *"Children learn to control their impulses by having rules imposed, then gradually learn to internalize those rules. Kids whose parents have never set limits often have difficulty controlling aggressive impulses, or even mustering the self-control to sit still in school." And a child who has never been allowed to feel frustration or pushed to do something he doesn't like is getting a dangerously lopsided view of the world . . .*
>
> *Adversity and frustration are an inevitable part of life, and to survive in the real world, you must know how to cope with them," says psychologist Diane Ehrensaft, Ph.D., author of* Spoiling Childhood. *"A parent who doesn't teach that skill isn't preparing her child for adulthood, and may be creating a self-centered, unpleasant person who will be unable to make the compromises necessary to establish solid relationships or get along with colleagues."*

A child who is disciplined will develop better self-discipline, an attribute that is vital to mature adult behavior. It is largely the responsibility of you, the parent, to see that discipline is carried out. Don't be a pushover parent.

Teach me to do your will, for you are my God;
may your good Spirit lead me on level ground.
PSALM 143:10

Finally, and perhaps most important, a child who has learned to obey his parents is more likely to choose to obey God.

"The wise in heart accept commands, but a chattering fool comes to ruin" (Proverbs 10:8).

"Hear, O Israel, and be careful to obey so that it may go well with you and that you may increase greatly in a land flowing with milk and honey, just as the Lord, the God of your fathers, promised you" (Deuteronomy 6:3).

"But Samuel replied: 'Does the Lord delight in burnt offerings and sacrifices as much as in obeying the voice of the Lord? To obey is better than sacrifice, and to heed is better than the fat of rams'" (1 Samuel 15:22).

"This is love for God: to obey his commands" (1 John 5:3).

Undoubtedly, choosing to obey God is a wise and wonderful choice. To reinforce that to your strong-willed child may take extensive time and energy. But that time and energy *is* well spent. Remember, the assumption that discipline does not work is untrue. The actuality is that the strong-willed child has an increased need for loving discipline. However, don't expect your strong-willed child to appreciate the discipline you administer, at least not when he is young and currently in the situation. Hopefully when he is an adult he will see the benefit of discipline. He may even choose to express his thanks to you. But in the early years don't look for it, expect it, or be disappointed if appreciation is not one of your child's responses to discipline. Remember, he is only a child.

Assumption vs. Actuality #3
Anomaly vs. Enormity in Number

The Lord made his people very fruitful;
he made them too numerous for their foes.
PSALM 105:24

Rather than an anomaly, a freak of nature, I discovered that the number of strong-willed children is quite prolific. I wonder how many are the oldest child in a family, presuming that their demanding nature might deter their parents from further family additions.

A multitude of parents tell me that they are relieved to discover that they are not alone. Their child is not the only one having a strong will. And consequently, there is help and hope.

It is a relief to realize that *your* strong-willed child is not the only one who acts the way he acts or thinks the way he thinks.

"I attended your seminar on strong-willed children at the Hearts at Home conference in November 2002. I listened to you with tears in my eyes because I can relate so well to everything you described."

I could map out a continuum to display the various perspectives on the role that discipline plays in a strong-willed child's life. One group of parents' view (and excuse for the lack of self-control a child exhibits) is summed up by the declaration "Of course he misbehaves. He's a strong-willed child." There is a great hazard in adopting this strategy. Being strong-willed is no more a justification for poor behavior than being a man or a woman or a blond or a redhead. Children do not need excuses for disrespectful conduct, they need parental discipline and encouragement of good behavior.

Others do not see the uniqueness of a strong-willed child and want to use the same methods with all children. I have heard, "None of *my* children are strong-willed." (That's possible.) And I've heard, "Don't you think that *all* children are strong-willed?" No, I don't. All children are children, with childish ways. They are not all strong-willed.

People with opinions on another point of the continuum view the pronouncement of a child as strong-willed equivalent to saying that he is bad. We all have strengths and weaknesses among our personality traits that are seemingly inherent. So does a strong-willed child. Some people might say that these children have more weaknesses than strengths, but I disagree.

"I am a strong-willed adult raising a strong-willed child. At a retreat, my husband was asked to name my best and worst qualities. 'Becky's best quality is that she is determined. Her worst is that she is pig-headed.' My son is teaching me how those can be the best and worst qualities in a person."

My favorite definition of a weakness is "A strength carried to extremes." I believe I first heard it from the lips of Florence Littauer, the author of *Personality Plus*.

"Face your deficiencies and acknowledge them; but do not let them master you. Let them teach you patience, sweetness, insight. When we do the best we can, we never know what miracle is wrought in our life, or in the life of another."[2]
HELEN KELLER

Think about the explanation that a weakness is a strength carried to extremes. On any given day, it is possible for any of us to take some wonderful, positive, God-given attribute and allow it to be carried to extremes, and it becomes a weakness.

Perhaps our youngest son, Jonathan, expressed it best. One evening Aaron, the strong-willed child turned adult, was describing a situation, which, to him, even as an adult, was very black-and-white. His passion and excitement were escalating as he gave his account. Finally, as he paused to take a breath, his younger brother sighed and said of that passionate, one-track thinking, "I know that's one of his better points, but sometimes I can't stand it."

Assumption vs. Actuality #4
Targeting You vs. Testing You

Don't be afraid to tell God exactly how you feel (He's already read your thoughts anyway).[3]
ELISABETH ELLIOT

The parents of a strong-willed child are prone to lose sleep trying to answer the question, "Why does this child hate me?" Relax and fall asleep—he doesn't hate you. He loves you. Your strong-willed child is not targeting you with his unrelenting challenges of your authority—he is testing you. He is curious to discover if you are *now* ready to relinquish control of him. Do you love him enough to hold your ground? After all, he is eager and willing to be in charge if you abdicate the throne. The stark difference between a strong-willed child and one who is not is that the strong-willed child will continually retest you. Winning one battle does not mean a victor is declared. Strong-willed children have more fortitude than most adults. And, unfortunately, too many parents give up before their strong-willed children do. They throw in the towel, and, in fact, no one is the winner.

Because a strong-willed child requires such high maintenance, and because he is more than aware of the extra energy his parents must exert, the possibility exists (at least in his mind) that his parents might give up. He thinks they might surrender and no longer be willing to go the extra mile (or two or three or four . . .) that is demanded in parenting a strong-willed child.

Furthermore, a strong-willed child often receives a smaller amount of positive strokes than a more compliant child. The strong-willed child is periodically irritating the adults in his life rather than pleasing them. He is hence more likely to test adults to see if they are still willing to show him love and be consistent by setting and reinforcing the boundaries.

"When it comes to relating to the strong-willed child, these [basic parenting] principles take on even more significance, since almost everything in the relationship—both positive and negative—tends to be more extreme."[4]

Cynthia Tobias

Because the strong-willed child is challenging, being his parent can be very tiring. It is easy to be exhausted and angry in the process of parenting. On more than one occasion, I found myself upset with Aaron and angry with myself for being upset with him. The continual testing and the numerous battles took a toll on my patience and my good attitude.

Interestingly, the majority of the notes that I receive from parents of strong-willed children either begin or end with a declaration of the parents' love for their difficult child. The rest of the note typically depicts an incredible strong-willed antic or adventure. Why do we (especially mothers) feel the need to announce our love for our strong-willed child? Because sometimes, even when we know we love him, we're not so sure we like him.

Your strong-willed child can make you very angry. In fact, the chances are great that he *will* make you angry. Why? It is because the antics of the strong-willed child are capable of embarrassing you as a parent. They confirm in the minds of others your inability to be the perfect parent.

"I love my son so much. He has so many good qualities. He is funny, and extremely energetic. He's athletic, loving, and confident in his abilities. I am a stay-at-home mom and have an absurdly difficult time having the energy to endure him every day. I do not think he will be starting kindergarten next year. His birthday is in May, and I want to see if one more year of maturity will help him to sit still in school. On the upside, I never get a complaint about him at preschool or when he goes to a friend's house. People think I make these stories up about him."

Still, a strong-willed child is exasperating and unashamedly irritating until control is gained. Those are the kinds of things that trigger anger. It's okay. What is not okay is to discipline in anger. Remember, your strong-willed child is not targeting you; he is testing you. Be sure to get an A on the test. Don't surrender to the pressure to give up and give in. Show him you love him by being the authority figure. You are not a target.

Therefore, since we are surrounded by such a great cloud of witnesses, let us throw off everything that hinders and the sin that so easily entangles, and let us run with perseverance the race marked out

*for us. Let us fix our eyes on Jesus, the author and perfecter of
our faith, who for the joy set before him endured the cross,
scorning its shame, and sat down at the right hand of the throne
of God. Consider him who endured such opposition from sinful men,
so that you will not grow weary and lose heart.*

HEBREWS 12:1–3

Assumption vs. Actuality #5
Prison vs. Presidency

*Let me tell you the secret that has led me to my goal.
My strength lies solely in my tenacity.*[5]

LOUIS PASTEUR

There is no doubt in the mind of the parents that their strong-willed child has determination. In fact, that word seems much too mild. A strong-willed child has determination combined with resolve and fortitude and stamina and good old-fashioned grit. The key for every parent is to focus that determination and to point it in a positive direction and not to let it be a roadblock on the journey. As James Dobson observes:

> *"It would appear that the strong-willed child may possess more character and have greater potential for a productive life than his compliant counterpart. However, the realization of that potential may depend on a firm but loving early home environment."*[6]

Debunking the assumption that the strong-willed child is en route to disaster has to do with how you, a significant adult in your child's life, handle your assignment of parenting. You are dealing with a persistent personality, and you must be able to stand firm. Strong-willed children are born leaders. That is not the issue. The question is, which group will they lead?

Will your strong-willed child find the cure for the suffering of cancer, or will his behavior create more pain and suffering in the world? Will he lead the youth group or the local gang? The research group or the chain gang?

Adolf Hitler announced to the German Army upon the assumption of its command, "After fifteen years of work I have achieved, as a common

German soldier and merely with my fanatical willpower, the unity of the German nation and have freed it from the death sentence of Versailles. My

"Leaders are ordinary people with extraordinary determination."[7]

ALIVE AND WELL IN THE FAST LANE

soldiers! You will understand, therefore, that my heart belongs entirely to you, that my will and my work unswervingly are serving the greatness of my and your nation, and that my mind and determination know nothing but annihilation of the enemy—that is to say, victorious termination of the [second world] war."[8]

Could there be a more disgusting representative of a will of iron being used for evil and not for good? The possibilities are endless, on both ends of the spectrum. However, the determination and leadership skills of a strong-willed child can most definitely work for his benefit.

"Our pediatrician said that these [strong-willed] children may one day grow up to find a cure for cancer, but you have to channel their strong will in the right direction."

"Our ten-year-old son, Ricky, had been friends with a boy in the neighborhood for years. Then one day he severed the relationship completely. Why? He discovered that the other boy was smoking marijuana. Ricky, a very strong-willed child, drew the line and would have nothing to do with something that he knew was wrong."

Assumption vs. Actuality #6
Average Inelligence vs. Above Average Intelligence

Wise men store up knowledge.
PROVERBS 10:14

One of the major pursuits of a strong-willed child is to gain or maintain control of his life. That is even more important to him than leading others. He does not want someone else to control him. In order to be successful in this pursuit, it is my contention that many strong-willed children possess above-average intelligence. I am not saying that every strong-willed child is a genius, and I am also not saying that every compliant child is dull. I do suggest the possibility that a strong-willed child, in order to create such chaos at times, must at least be ingenious. Trust me—the supposition that a strong-willed child is bright will NOT necessarily manifest itself in the academic world (at least not right away). Still, anyone who can get the best of an adult who is potentially twenty-five or more years older must be bright.

It would seem that this child was thinking, "What can I say to motivate my parents to give in to my wishes? Ah, I know! I'll use guilt, a highly effective weapon in the battle for control." This child was bright enough to choose an appropriate weapon from his arsenal.

"When Brian was little, he could be quite a challenge. When he signed up for high school wrestling, God gave me a peek into why He'd created Brian that way. All of that strong-willed energy went into his left shoulder, which would not hit the mat. I was so grateful for that insight and for God's keeping me from thinking it was necessary to unstrung my son. Today he is an engineer. I'm thankful for strong-willed engineers for they are the ones who build our homes, bridges, and world. May they never cave in to anyone's negative pressure, no matter who it is from."

Let's return, for a minute, to the scene of the coup that Aaron organized in elementary school. John and I did not know about it until the fateful meeting with his teacher. I discovered much later that at least one of my good friends was not in the dark about the goings-on in this particular classroom. Jackie, one of Aaron's school friends, was one of the classmates who boycotted the journaling assignment at Aaron's recommendation. Probably a year after this incident, her mother and I were chatting. (I'm guessing it was at least a year, because that is how long it took me to cope with the shock and embarrassment of his takeover.) When I asked Kay if she knew about the incident, she gently admitted that she did. And then she added her daughter Jackie's analysis of the situation: "Jackie told me that Aaron really *should* be in charge because, and I quote, 'He is much smarter than our teacher!'"

"Peter was making the transition into first grade. We pulled up to school when he declared that he did not want to go to school, and he was NOT going to go to school. As we walked toward the front door of the school he looked at me and said, 'I thought you were going to homeschool me.'"

So, is Jackie's evaluation the basis for my idea that the strong-willed child is typically a bright and creative child, an out-of-the-box thinker? No, more than the opinion of one loyal friend is the realization that many strong-willed children have managed to gain control of adults, one or even two generations older.

"The class was told that they had forty minutes to complete the true/false test. This test was not for a grade. The results would simply be recorded in each student's permanent record. Ian decided that this was a silly waste of time. Being a creative, strong-willed child, he decided to challenge himself by purposefully answering each question wrong.

When the test was graded and scored, he had earned a 2%. Wow! Actually he had gotten 98% correct—well,

---

sort of. Try explaining that one to his teacher. The permanent record reported a score of 2%."

Because of their ability to solve (as well as create) problems, it is wise to give a strong-willed child responsibility that is age appropriate. By giving him a worthwhile task to do, it builds up his sense of worth and allows him to develop credibility in his own mind. Putting trust in your strong-willed child to do the job assigned to him validates his abilities and illustrates your confidence in him. It is also important to assist him to realize, even at an early age, how important it is to align himself with positive people of good character. Encourage your strong-willed child to accept responsibility for himself in other arenas also. This can help him feel significant and keep him on the path most destined for success.

A Closer Look with Aaron

As a grown man, looking back to my days as a strong-willed child, I am certain that I was most impacted by the assumption that I was tough and not tender. I realized that this assumption was incorrect when I realized that I could replay in detail so many of the hurtful experiences that resulted from my strong-willed nature. I know that my older and younger brothers had unpleasant things happen to them in their growing-up years, things that seemed unfair or cruel, and the chance exists that their episodes were no less painful than mine. The difference is that in most cases they cannot vividly recall the incidents, issues, or the intensity of the episodes. I can.

There were definitely repercussions from when my strong-willed nature got out of control. At those times, I knew that what I was doing was wrong and that I was misbehaving. In spite of that admission, it is hard to imagine that some of the treatment that I received from one or two noteworthy adults was justifiable. The fact that I can remember dramatic details, like an out-of-control classmate being allowed (and in a sense, encouraged) to spit on me, is an illustration of the pain it caused.

Parents, your strong-willed child is hoping, no, begging, for you to take and maintain control and to comfort him when the world lashes back in what they think is self-defense. This does not come in the form of justifying his inappropriate behavior. It is in acknowledging his mistake and granting him grace to grow and mature; the grace he requires to move forward and learn more about how to control his strong-willed nature. He needs you to show your love for him by being his parent, not his friend or his oppressor.

Being strong-willed may be programmed from birth, but each time a "strength is carried to extremes," it is a conscious decision. It is not a reflex. We are waging war, partly with our own strong emotions. Please come to our rescue by loving us enough to help us learn proper control—godly self-control of our actions and emotions. We will test you and almost everyone. We are looking for adults who are patient and persistent in their love. We want you to be willing to invest your time, energy, emotion, and love in us.

A Good Word from John, the Resident Dad

The false assumption that bothers me the most is that these strong-willed kids are as tough as nails. That is so far from the truth. The strong-willed child is actually tender-hearted. The sensitive nature of a strong-willed child, however, is often overlooked or discounted by other children and also by adults.

In junior high school, Aaron was tagged by a teacher with a nickname insinuating that he was not coordinated. It was not flattering. In fact, a T-shirt was printed with that name on the back—a T-shirt that was to be worn at the school club meetings. Aaron's feelings were hurt, but he was helpless to change the situation. The teacher assumed that he was tough enough to handle the teasing. She made that assumption based, no doubt, on his opinionated nature as a strong-willed child. She was wrong in her assumption and it took a trip to school to explain that he'd need a different T-shirt with something more positive on the back. Parents, in a situation like this it is appropriate to intervene as an advocate.

The more good decisions Aaron was able to make, the fewer the incorrect assumptions people made about him as a strong-willed child. That doesn't mean they were eliminated by the high school years. At the end of his freshman year in high school I was once again privy to an adult assuming that Aaron was tough and not tender. It was the end of a sports season and an awards evening was announced. Aaron informed us that he did not want to attend the recognition event even though he had earned a letter and it would be awarded that evening. I could not imagine why he was so reluctant and I encouraged him to change his mind. After some positive persuasion, Aaron said he would go. After the evening was over, I realized why Aaron was not enthusiastic about going and I felt very bad for influencing him to attend.

The coach said a few words about each of the athletes and even though they were essentially positive comments, there was a hint of sarcasm in each of his "tributes." When he got to Aaron, the sarcasm was more than a hint. He awarded Aaron a varsity letter and also words of discouragement. On the ride home I apologized for not understanding what Aaron had been almost sure would, and did, transpire.

I am very certain that the assumption that bothers me the most is the incorrect view these strong-willed kids are as tough as nails. That is far from the truth.

My strong-willed child and yours are actually tender-hearted.

CHAPTER FIVE

The Junior High Journey

*Adolescence is an awesome
and sacred time of life—
it is not a disease to be cured.*[1]
WAYNE RICE

Junior high is a time of change for every young man and woman. For our strong-willed child, it was time for a fresh start. Aaron was changing buildings, administrators, and class structure—and hopefully changing and maturing in the ability to control his strong-willed ways. Junior high provided him with increased opportunities for responsibility. Now he could join student council, various sports teams, drama, and special music groups. There was more diversity in the classes that were offered, with different students making up each one.

For us as the parents of a strong-willed child, the junior high years were still a time of guiding, encouraging, correcting, and molding. The job was not finished just because Aaron reached his teen years. While there were no more classroom coups, there were still incorrect decisions resulting from his strong-willed nature.

Again, Aaron intersected with some wonderful, encouraging adults and, again, occasional roadblocks. Perhaps one of the most encouraging situations actually occurred at church. Aaron was the only student in the junior high Sunday school class. In fact, his individualized instruction went even further. He had not one, but two teachers. A husband and wife team, Lawrence and Loretta, taught the class.

We always thank God for all of you,
mentioning you in our prayers.
We continually remember before our God and Father
your work produced by faith,
your labor prompted by love,
and your endurance inspired by hope
in our Lord Jesus Christ.
1 THESSALONIANS 1:2–3

Do you find it unusual that these two adults would *both* commit to a single junior high school boy? It might seem more reasonable if one of them had opted out of the instructor's role. (Or maybe even both of

"Lord, change me."
EVELYN CHRISTENSON

them.) After all, Aaron could always go up to the high school class or down to the class for fifth and sixth graders. Everyone would understand and be supportive. But that wasn't the case. These two wonderful Christian people gave Aaron their undivided attention Sunday after Sunday.

Because he was the solo student, his questions never disrupted the rest of the class members. On any particular Sunday, Aaron, Lawrence, and Loretta might begin in Genesis and end up somewhere in the New Testament, pursuing one of the mysteries that caught Aaron's attention.

Lawrence and Loretta encouraged Aaron's questions and spiritual growth. They were not put off by his desire to set his own course. Instead they were willing to navigate that course with him.

As the parent of a strong-willed child, it is important that you search for adults who are capable of and willing to affirm your son or daughter. I have discovered that being kind and respectful to the children at church is an important calling for every adult, but some are more enthusiastic than others about that proposition. If you discover that your child is in an environment that is hostile (because of the adult's natural attitude or the adult's reaction to your child), I would recommend that you find different surroundings.

As a frequent speaker at *Hearts at Home* conferences and a contributor to their magazine, I am asked many questions about family relationships. One day I received an e-mail from a mother about a problem that revolved around her daughter. It seemed that this girl "was picked on" by the students, and ultimately the teacher, in the public school that she attended. The parent withdrew her daughter from this school and entered her in a private, Christian school. Before long, the same pattern of behavior began. Her daughter was once again "being picked on," and the teacher was again a negative part of the mix. The mother's question to me was, "Do you think I should homeschool my daughter? Everywhere we go, she is singled out for criticism."

My reply was probably not what this mother was expecting. I assured her that in spite of the rough times her daughter was experiencing, there was some possible good to be found in the situations. Both schools, both groups of students, both teachers responded to her daughter in the same way. The variables were the schools, the students, and the teachers. The constant was her daughter. That was, in a very real sense, the good news. Why? Because this mother still had the chance to positively influence the behavior of her daughter. Her opportunity to control any of the other factors was slim. I suggested that perhaps it was her daughter's behavior that was the problem, behavior that could hopefully be modified by the mother.

In this case, I did NOT recommend finding an alternative environment. If your child is creating and re-creating a hostile setting, it is time to work with your child, not with others.

For nothing is impossible with God.
LUKE 1:37

The junior high years brought another positive encourager into Aaron's life. In third grade, Aaron was finally given a horse. The lobbying for this creature began near the time Aaron started talking. For years we held him off by explaining that there was already one horse on his grandfather's farm down the road, and one horse was enough. The fact that this horse was old and decrepit and seemed to have a death wish for anyone who dared to saddle it, didn't influence our decision. We were NOT going to buy another horse while that one was alive. Speaking of a death wish, I would not be surprised if Aaron's prayers included a petition for God to "get rid of Fury" as soon as possible. Eventually, Fury did die, and that gave Aaron the green light to push for a "decent horse."

Aaron's grandfather purchased Lady, the new horse, later that year. As a six-year-old mare she was big, but not too big for Aaron. He spent hour after hour with Lady, one day literally investing three hours in coaxing her to take a bit. He was inordinately patient with her (something he seldom was with human beings). When Lady reached her two-year anniversary of living on the farm, Aaron announced that she was lonely and that "being a social animal" she needed another horse for companionship. My recollection is that the answer was a firm, "No one is buying another horse." When you live on a working farm, you may have the space for multiple horses, but most animals are expected to be productive and not just for entertainment.

Aaron, our strong-willed, out-of-the-box thinker, came up with a plan so that he could have his way and not ask anyone to invest money in the purchase of another horse. By this time, we were friends with Ed, the owner of several horses. Ed and his family lived about ten miles away. His middle son and our eldest son, Matthew, were very good friends. They played together on sports teams from junior high on, and because of that, the lives of our two families intersected.

One day Aaron approached Ed with a plan. "If I can earn enough money, can I pay you to have your stallion breed my mare?" And Ed's reply? "I'll let our stallion stay with your mare if you will break him before he comes back home. I won't charge you a stud fee if you won't charge me to break the stallion." What a *terrific* deal! As far as Aaron was concerned, it was a huge win-win—for him! If everything went as planned, he would have two horses, his mare and a foal, *and* he would have the fun of breaking Ed's horse! Dad agreed and everything went as planned. Duchess, the foal, was born in about a year, and the stallion, named SW, was broken and trained in great fashion.

That first partnership began a long relationship. By the time Aaron was in junior high, he was breaking horses for Ed on a regular basis and also learning how to sell them. I once heard him say, "I try to treat my horses the way I want adults to treat me. I care about their well-being and am patient with them, but they don't get away with any disobedience!" Aaron's horses were therapeutic for him. And so was his relationship with Ed—an adult who respected Aaron's abilities, gave him responsibility, and taught him how to be a "horse trader" in the very best sense of the phrase.

In today's society, those of us who live on a farm are in the minority. In fact, we now represent less than 3 percent of the population. So what take-home value is there from this positive scenario for those of you who do not have a bale of hay within twenty miles? The key here is not necessarily the horse itself. It is the *responsibility* that Aaron was allowed, encouraged actually, to accept. How can that be replicated in the city? One option is smaller animals. If your son or daughter desires to have a pet, this can be a great opportunity for responsibility—so can a paper route or any other part-time job. Be sure that *you* aren't assuming the responsibility, however. That defeats the purpose.

Don't let anyone look down on you
because you are young,
but set an example for the believers
in speech, in life, in love, in faith and in purity.
1 TIMOTHY 4:12

Another positive influence in Aaron's junior high journey was his principal. One of Aaron's passions is politics. He is interested in it today and was interested in it in junior high school. This interest was fueled by discussions with willing adults like his junior high principal. He and Aaron came from opposite ends of the political spectrum. When the daily news contained a controversial political issue, Mr. Burkey would seek out Aaron and ask his spin on the current event. One day when Aaron was in eighth grade, we received a letter from the principal's office. (Now *that* can bring terror into the heart of any strong-willed child's parent.) In the letter, Mr. Burkey complimented Aaron on his sound grasp of national issues and his ability to debate those issues confidently and from an informed position. The principal also commented on the maturity with which Aaron listened to a differing point of view. (I do believe that I saved that note! In fact, I might have even mounted it in a scrapbook!)

What was Mr. Burkey doing? He was allowing Aaron to share his views in a controlled environment and encouraging him to think. Never did he say, "I'm much too busy and important to discuss things with *you*, a junior high boy." No, instead, he enjoyed the banter and debate with a young man who was learning to express himself and, more important, learning to listen to others' opinions.

Do you ever take the time to encourage your child to express himself? Are you interested in his thoughts and opinions? All too often, we as the overtired, disheartened parents of strong-willed children do not encourage our children to think and to express themselves, especially if they do not walk in lockstep with our thinking. When was the last time you engaged your adolescent strong-willed child in a conversation about something *he* was interested in? Why are our "conversations" more like reading an instruction manual? "Do this and then do this. And whatever you do, don't do that!" Or we talk simply to discover facts. "What time does the bus leave? Did you tell Chad we would pick him up?" Your strong-willed child's journey will be enhanced if you look for ways to converse with him about *his* interests.

> *Fathers, do not exasperate your children;*
> *instead, bring them up in the*
> *training and instruction of the Lord.*
> EPHESIANS 6:4

By junior high school, it is necessary for parents to develop alternative ways to discipline their strong-willed child. Obviously as children mature, it becomes inappropriate to spank. The hope is that, by this time in their lives, it is no longer necessary. But discipline will undoubtedly still be needed on occasion. There are several disciplinary measures that are effective with adolescents. The loss of independence or the suspensions of recreational activities (i.e., limiting or prohibiting computer play, television, or time on the phone with friends) are, when necessary, very effective means of control as a child gets older. How do you determine the appropriate discipline? You go back to the basics. Number one, you must be able to enforce any discipline you threaten. Number two, you must be certain that the discipline will be effective. Ask yourself, what occupies my child's free time? What does he enjoy doing? If you choose to limit his access to something he is genuinely interested in, your discipline will be effective.

Usually, by junior high school, the way a strong-willed child maintains control has also matured and developed. A friend who is one of my favorite examples of a strong-willed child turned responsible adult, told me that his most successful weapon of control in the junior and senior high years was his use of humor. After all, how could someone punish a person who brought such great laughter and delight to the scene? Although this was not a ploy used extensively by our strong-willed child, I can understand how it could be effective.

I already told you that it was not completely smooth sailing by junior high school. There were still some roadblocks along the way. Like another teacher who decided that Aaron's "creative alternative" to her instruction was *rebellion* and that it must be squelched with force as soon as possible. (Can you guess that we did not agree with her reaction?) In this instance, a trip to school was made to get the precise facts. During our visit, the teacher calmed down and actually admitted that even if Aaron did have a legitimate suggestion, she was not willing to examine it. (As my own father used to say, "Don't confuse me with the facts. My mind is made up!") How's that for being flexible and adapting to circumstances? We explained to Aaron that she was the teacher, he was the student, and she had more power. We also let him know that, in our opinion, she was wrong and he was right. Although we did not agree with her stance, we told Aaron that he would have to comply. This woman was an adult and his teacher, and he had to treat her with respect whether or not he respected all of her judgments.

This was a teachable moment for Aaron. Life is not fair. We were able to persuade Aaron to let go of some battles—something that he would have to do throughout life, even as an adult. Part of his willingness to comply was fueled by the fact that we talked honestly with him. The truth is very powerful. Just because this woman was the teacher and an adult did not make her correct. She merely held a position that was to be respected. If we had failed to examine the situation correctly and instead made a blanket statement that she was right and Aaron was wrong, he would have had a more difficult time giving up control.

Jesus said, "If you hold to my teaching,
you are really my disciples.
Then you will know the truth,
and the truth will set you free."
JOHN 8:31–32

In this case, the "truth" was twofold. The teacher had made a poor decision, and it was in Aaron's best interest to comply. That truth set Aaron free to acquiesce and move forward. Learning that "the better part of valor is discretion," is an important lesson from Shakespeare for a strong-willed child.[2] As the parent of a strong-willed child, it is imperative that you are honest and straightforward with him. Try to avoid assuming a position on either end of the continuum. It is incorrect to *always* conclude that your strong-willed child is right. That is one radical end of the spectrum. The other is to determine that you must protect any and all unsuspecting adults from your strong-willed child, always making him the bad guy, the one at fault. Neither extreme is valuable. Each situation must be scrutinized and evaluated. Search for the truth and do not be reluctant to share it with your child. If you are willing to handle each conflict one by one, with wisdom and fairness, your strong-willed child is more likely to acknowledge your appraisal and act accordingly.

A Closer Look with Aaron

I like absolutes. I believe that is true for the majority of us who are strong-willed. In junior high, life begins to become less and less "absolute," less black-and-white. As teachers introduce more topics and issues that can be interpreted as gray, they also give opinions. It is quite possible that the opinions presented (sometimes even presented as fact) will not reinforce the standards you have for your family.

It is necessary for the parents of a junior high strong-willed child to be honest with him at all times and in every instance. At this stage, topics are more thought-provoking and more controversial. We strong-willed children really do love a world that is black-and-white. We thrive on absolutes. In junior high school and beyond, the world is shouting that there are many, many gray areas.

God's Word has absolute truths that need to be reinforced with even more enthusiasm as the world strives to make His truths subjective. I remember discussions about creation, gender differences, morality, and tolerance of others' beliefs (not necessarily the Christian's) being prolific in the junior high years. I am not saying that we should relinquish thinking and evaluation of situations that are truly gray in nature. I am saying that junior high is the time to live by the straightforward truth of the Bible.

We had a ritual in our home, one that always existed as far as I know. When Mom or Dad said prayers with us at night they always concluded by making a statement and then asking a question. "Mom and Dad love you lots and lots. And who loves you best?" That was our cue to holler, "Jesus!" We did it night after night by memory. We didn't have to contemplate that question. The answer was always the same. It was a ritual—a habit—our nighttime routine. And the truth! By junior high we were on our own with our evening prayers, but that truth was firmly planted in our minds and hearts.

What would have happened if my parents' words and actions had not been in sync? Obviously, I would have believed their actions. I'm not trying to suggest that they never messed up or made mistakes. Of course they did. But their desire was to live the truth and to encourage all of their children to do the same.

In junior high school, an adolescent becomes more aware of varying lifestyles, thoughts, and standards of behavior. More and more viewpoints are introduced, with the majority of them contrasting the basics of Christianity. I suppose that if your child is enrolled in a Christian school, this conflict may be slightly postponed. But for those who attend a public school, junior high is a place where values are questioned.

When I was growing up, there was a quote on the wall of one of the Sunday school rooms that read: "If you don't stand for something, you'll fall for anything." What are the basic beliefs and standards of your family? Do you live by them, or do you just espouse them? Your strong-willed child is watching you. Do you encourage your strong-willed child to tell the truth, and then you tell the person on the other end of the phone that your spouse, sitting in the family room, is not home? Every junior high child needs the assurance of your constancy, your black-and-white behavior. For example, my dad never swore. There was no question in my mind about whether something could push him over the edge and cause him to change. He was constant. And his example was something I could count on and a pattern that I could replicate.

Parents, it is also important to know *why* you have taken a stand. The strong-willed child wants to know why. My compliant brothers probably had no problem giving in when the explanation to the order was "because I said so." That was never enough for me. Be ready to substantiate your conviction.

If your strong-willed child wants an explanation of why "We're all going to church," the correct answer is NOT "because I said so," nor is it "because if we don't go to church, we'll go to hell." That's not the truth. Why DO you want your junior high child to go to church? Can you answer his question about this or any other conviction you may have? Be prepared! Now is the time to "walk your talk" more than ever before! That will help your child trust you and accept your appraisal of situations and recommendations of how to handle those situations.

Value his intelligence. Have legitimate conversations with him. Just because he is an adolescent does not mean that he does not need your input or that he will disregard it. He has a strong desire to know the absolutes found in God's Word and have them reinforced by his loving parent. This will help him as he comes to his own conclusions about some of the legitimately gray areas. And it will help him articulate his own convictions.

I met a young man whose parents were of two different races. Their child was completely Caucasian in his looks, with blond hair and blue eyes. When he studied genetics in junior high science and learned about recessive and dominant genes, the question arose in his mind, "How could I have inherited such Aryan looks when the other race is dominant?" It was then that he learned that one parent was not his biological parent. The lie that had been accepted as truth for years led to extreme pain in this family.

I've often wondered if the children who are told that Santa Claus is real question other things that their parents have said. Is Jesus real? Be honest with your children, especially with your strong-willed one. Allow your strong-willed child to ask questions. In fact, encourage legitimate questions. Yes, there are gray areas in life. Help your child understand which areas those are. Let him ask questions, and then try your best to answer them. It is important to him.

A Good Word from John, the Resident Dad

Junior high—those two words evoke fear in the lives of many parents. It is because the junior high years are times of great transition. Boys and girls alike are moving from childhood into adulthood with the process typically being two steps forward and one step backward. This time of great change can be difficult for both parents and their kids.

The changes that occur in the lives of these young teenagers are not only physical, and emotional, but also situational. The environment of the classroom changes in junior high and middle school, and assignments demand more self-discipline and responsibility. On the physical and emotional level, bodies are changing rapidly and so are the temptations associated with those changes. All this adds up to more and more decisions that will have to be made. And with these young teens seeking autonomy and independence, more decisions will be made without initially consulting you as the parents.

This uncertain time of increased freedom can actually equate to an increased opportunity for the strong-willed child to stand up for what is right—an opportunity to shine.

At the age of thirteen, Aaron was on a three-day trip for a

school-sponsored event. The kids were assigned roommates, and he shared a room with two guys he had known for years. During the evening on the second night in the hotel, one of the boys displayed a "girlie magazine" he had brought from home. Aaron told him in no uncertain terms that he needed to put it away; that he shouldn't have brought it on the trip in the first place.

I am almost certain that the boy with the magazine was shocked by Aaron's response. What he did not realize was that Aaron would be intolerant of looking at the magazine. Aaron was certain that looking at scantily-clad women was NOT a good idea. Aaron was the only roommate who took a stand. He was not the only one who knew it was wrong. But the more compliant roommate, the other young man assigned to that room, did not see the necessity of causing a commotion. A strong-willed child is more than willing to cause a commotion in order to right a wrong.

I was not consulted prior to Aaron's decision to enforce the rules he knew were correct. The basis of his decision, however, had been cultivated long before that evening. As parents, that is our responsibility. Our job is to be certain we have helped our children learn what is right and have the courage to do what is right.

How do we do that as parents? How do you help your children learn what is right?

The primary answer is to realize the importance of introducing your child to the Word of God, the love of God, the power of God, and the fear of God. This is done by exposure to good Bible teaching at church and in your own home. In addition, it is accomplished by you becoming a living illustration to your child. When we do our best as parents to be men and women of character, knowing that what is done in secret is no secret to God, we are teaching our children to be men and women of character.

Recently our pastor did a series entitled "An Audience of One," about the life and witness of Daniel. Daniel, an Israelite taken into captivity in Babylon, is a wonderful illustration of doing what is right. He refused to eat food that God had declared unclean knowing the refusal might cost him his life. Our kids need to see us living for an audience of one, standing up for what is right. That is necessary for every child and especially for the strong-willed child.

Strong-willed children are willing to take the risk to do what should be done

The fact that Aaron accepted our decision about how to handle an unwavering, inflexible teacher marked a great move toward maturity. It also indicated to us that some of the goals we had as parents were being met. It is important that the parents of strong-willed children set goals to mark the journey, determine the desired destination, and plot progress toward that end.

"As your kids get older, LOOSEN your grip on things that have no lasting moral significance, and TIGHTEN your grip on things that do."[3]
WAYNE RICE

CHAPTER SIX

Determining the Desired Destination

*I press on toward the goal to win the prize
for which God has called me
heavenward in Christ Jesus.*
PHILIPPIANS 3:14

The strong-willed child is not without a goal. From the beginning, the goal of a strong-willed child is to be in control of his life. And he pursues that goal with determination and gusto, needing little outside motivation or stimulus. Unfortunately, being in control is not always in his best interest. That is why you, as the parent of a strong-willed child, need to develop goals for his journey.

Setting goals for your strong-willed child can be tricky business. Remember, the strong-willed child desires to be in control of his own life. If you set goals for him, you are, in a very real sense, seeking to control him. The strong-willed child who gets an inkling of the idea that his parents are directing him this way or that way, is likely to turn around and go in the opposite direction.

So do you still set goals? Absolutely! But these are definitely not shared with your strong-willed child. In a sense, these are actually goals for the parents. They are set to guide them as they shape the journey of their strong-willed child.

First of all, as parents, we wanted Aaron to know in his heart, not just his head, that Jesus loved him and that He wanted the very best for him. That was the most important goal. Our goals had to be specific, attainable, and measurable. A specific goal was that Aaron would accept Christ as his Savior at an early age, and the sooner the better. This was both specific and attainable. It was measurable by his proclamation of the decision and subsequent behavior. In order to facilitate this goal, we attended Sunday school and church each Sunday. We read the Bible to the kids each day and prayed as a family at breakfast. We prayed with Aaron each night before bedtime. And we accepted the challenge to do what was by far the most difficult and the most powerful thing— to live our faith before him each day (to walk our talk), not perfectly, but with conviction and with love. There is no formula to guarantee that a child will accept the love of God and become a Christian, but it is a goal worthy of every attempt made to encourage it.

> *"The man who walks with God always gets to his destination."*[1]
>
> HENRIETTA MEARS

With the help of God's Holy Spirit, the strong-willed child begins to understand that using his strengths negatively and in destructive ways isn't the best plan. Winning at the expense of another is not what Christ supports or applauds.

> *When I was a child, I talked like a child,*
> *I thought like a child, I reasoned like a child.*
> *When I became a man, I put childish ways behind me.*
> 1 CORINTHIANS 13:11

We also determined that it would be attainable and very positive if, by the end of junior high school, Aaron had the skills to make consistently good decisions without our direct coaching, reactive intervention, or punishment. After all, when a child is only nine years old he is halfway to adulthood and being able to live on his own. If we missed our self-imposed deadline of Aaron's exit from junior high, we still had a little time (high school) to be a direct, daily influence in his life. Specifically, we hoped to observe Aaron choosing not to battle for his own way with authority figures, but to be mature even when dealing with immature adults. We would measure this by his behavior and reports from him and his teachers.

Obviously, we desired for Aaron to ultimately use his gifts and talents to be a productive member of society. We wanted to help him evaluate other people's input (positive and negative), teaching him to apply it to his life when it was relevant and reject it if it was not godly input. It is important to take criticism or comments of any kind "straight to the top" to the Lord, the Creator of strengths and the Corrector of weaknesses. It is important to teach your child to be discerning. If someone's purpose is merely to discourage your strong-willed child and convince him that he is less than who he really is in Christ Jesus, that person's opinion is not to be valued. If, on the other hand, the suggestions or criticisms have validity, it is time to prayerfully work for change.

"Inch by inch, it's a cinch."

UNKNOWN

Aaron's achievement of the majority of these goals was *almost* attained by the end of junior high. The important thing to remember about most goals is that even if you don't hit the bull's-eye each time, you are much closer than you would have been without the establishment of goals in the first place.

Reaching the goals we set was not an overnight accomplishment. I will be the first to admit that in this age of instant mashed potatoes and e-mail, I am not very good at delayed gratification. So, how do you continue the process when it seems to take so long?

First of all, it is important to assess your starting point and, if at all possible, begin the process of moving forward immediately. By noting your starting point, all progress can be celebrated. As soon as we recognized that Aaron was a high-maintenance child, we began to look for ways to help him use his strong-willed nature in positive ways. The fact that Aaron took control of his grade school classroom and organized a coup was certainly an indicator that we still had ground to cover, but it was not a step backward. Helping a strong-willed child learn to temper his strong-willed nature and make good choices is a process—a long and sometimes arduous process—but a process necessary to facilitate his journey. It is like building a retaining wall of brick, a ten-story retaining wall, brick by brick. Aaron's coup did not pull bricks from under the structure, it merely indicated that the wall was still under construction. As much as we could, we would help Aaron become a good decision maker by the end of junior high.

We would help him construct that retaining wall, the wall that would hold back his strong emotion and the overwhelming desire to control his circumstances so that his journey could continue in a positive, forward manner. In order to reach that goal, we monitored his classroom behavior (with even more zeal after his successful grade school takeover). I didn't want to be surprised by a teary phone call from a teacher again! Undoubtedly, in the past I ignored some obvious indicators and just hoped for the best, which will not suffice for a strong-willed child. By keeping in closer communication with his teachers, we could intervene and help modulate his behavior when necessary, before the situation was out of control (and he was completely in control).

"Have patience. Have patience.

Don't be in such a hurry.

When you get impatient,

you only start to worry.

Remember. Remember.

That God is patient, too.

And think of all the times

when others had to wait for you!"[2]

THE MUSIC MACHINE

Whenever it was suitable, we dialoged with Aaron about what behavior was appropriate and what was not. We did not automatically agree or disagree with his behavior, but we tried to help him come to mature conclusions about what action would be most beneficial.

I remember talking with Aaron about a particular interaction with a group of his peers in junior high school. He attempted to control not only himself but the entire situation, when he deemed the behavior of his peers to be in error. Was he correct in his estimation of his friends' behavior? Yes, I believe he was. Was he positively influencing his friends with his abrupt, immovable response to their behavior? No, he was alienating them. As I recall, my exact words to him were, "It doesn't matter if you are right and everyone hates you. You haven't made a difference." Diplomacy is something a strong-willed child must cultivate. I am not suggesting that the strong-willed child give in to destructive, life-threatening choices or allow them in others' lives. But that was not the case in Aaron's particular situation. I am suggesting that the strong-willed child think through his motivation for (and method of) confronting and desiring to control others.

Little by little, brick by brick, we witnessed that retaining wall of discernment growing taller. We applauded Aaron's progress. Parents should always look for opportunities to catch their children doing something right. When his choices were not as good, we punished him if necessary and helped him determine what might have been a better route to take.

How did we know that we did not reach our parenting goal by the end of junior high? Because he still failed to comply with a teacher whose request was, in his way of thinking, silly. And his decision to maintain his own control in that instance resulted in a trip to the principal's office. Was the trip worth it? The strong-willed boy thought it was. After all, the teacher's demand was obviously frivolous. But was the trip worth it? We, the parents of that strong-willed boy, did NOT think it was.

> *"The most important single ingredient in the formula of success is knowing how to get along with people."*[3]
> THEODORE ROOSEVELT

Aaron could have made the choice to follow the rule, silly or not, and avoid the punishment. He had not "arrived" at the desired destination by then, but progress was still being made. The retaining wall was growing taller, and that was facilitating forward progress.

The first semester in high school, Aaron chose to get a B in a class in which he could have easily earned an A. Why? Again, his ultimate desire was for control. He decided that he could get an adequate grade without doing the work assigned. (It's rather interesting to me that he managed to receive no worse than a B.) The B grade was not as much the issue as was his choice not to do the work. We were disappointed in his decision, but the retaining wall was still getting closer to completion.

By the sophomore year, Aaron was making good choices with great consistency. And we were not involved in direct coaching, reactive intervention, or punishment. That is not to say that he never again made a poor choice. The difference was that he was now evaluating his own behavior and making necessary adjustments. We saw definite signs that he was tempering his wonderful gift of a strong-willed nature. The retaining wall was now complete to our specifications, and it was doing its job of holding back Aaron's desire for control at all costs.

Even though it is not a good idea to push your goals on another person, especially your strong-willed child, it is not a bad idea to help your child establish his own vision. The well-known proverb "Where there is no vision, the people perish" is derived from Proverbs 29:18. I have always broadly applied this verse to encourage young people, in my own home and in the youth group at our church, to establish a vision— a goal—a target on the wall. I challenged them to picture where they would like to be in ten years or what they would like to be doing. It is my theory that when this is done, when a vision is established, youth are much less likely to engage in activities which will hamper the achievement of those goals. Remember our Easter weekend visitor, Nathan, who told his parents about the dream he had to be a pilot and a farmer? That vision demanded certain things (like the successful completion of seventh grade). Defining his vision could help give him the motivation to accomplish the necessary task at hand, a task that was an essential step to seeing that vision accomplished.

> *"When we set exciting worthwhile goals for ourselves, they work in two ways:*
> *We work on them, and they work on us."*[4]
> EDGE LEARNING

Recently I discovered an exercise Aaron completed in grade school, a fill-in-the-blank. "When I grow up, I want to be a _____." And scribbled in the blank was the word "vet" (a veterinarian). Today he has accomplished that dream. It was his vision, his goal, and his self-determined target on the wall. It kept him from myriad poor choices that could have made his dream "perish." Help your strong-willed child determine his vision. Your ability to do that will be based on your relationship with your child. It is difficult to help someone achieve his goal or even *define* his goal if you do not truly know the individual. Be sure your strong-willed child knows of your great interest in him as a unique human being.

The strong-willed child is not interested in your vision for him. Your vision is for you and you alone. Don't be discouraged if you do not hit the bull's-eye right away or even if you do not hit it at all. The benefit of establishing a goal, of drawing a target on the wall, is that regardless of whether you hit the exact center of the target, at least you are facing the right wall!

> *"In absence of clearly defined goals, we become strangely loyal to performing daily acts of trivia."*
> UNKNOWN

A Closer Look with Aaron

Reflecting on the content of this particular chapter is by far the most difficult for me. Why? It is because I had no idea that my parents had a plan or a goal that they were trying to accomplish. And that is very good. I can't stress enough the importance of the parents of a strong-willed child functioning as a team, seriously evaluating their starting point and their finish line, and NOT sharing that information with their child. My folks were both good communicators, but they did not communicate their goals with me.

The idea that my parents had set goals for guiding my journey was a complete shock to me. I discovered that the day of Easter vacation, when I walked in on the family room discussion about raising a strong-willed child. Mom told you that I surprised her with some of my stories, stories of my strong-willed nature out of control. Well, she and Dad surprised me when I heard them tell our friends about setting specific goals. They shared with Nathan's parents their hopes that, by the end of junior high school, I would be consistently exercising control of my strong-willed disposition. I was stunned! They had a game plan. They had an undisclosed objective! Why was that necessary? Weren't we on the same team?

The realization that they had a strategy was astounding to me. In fact, when I became aware of that, I also became aware that I must have demanded a great deal of their energy. Believe it or not, that never occurred to me before. Later that weekend, I had one of my last strong-willed child "implosions" as I realized the truth of how difficult I must have been to parent. I got very emotional and, in a sense, felt detached from my two biggest supporters. My parents and I must have been on opposite teams! They had a plan, a strategy, a plot, and I was not privy to it. On Easter Sunday, late in the day, we had a discussion about what I recently discovered.

The truth was that we were NOT on opposing teams. We were on the same team. It was just that they were the cocaptains of the team, setting the game plan, and I was a player who didn't need that much information. They knew that the possibility existed that if I knew about their goals, I would go in exactly the opposite direction—just for the sake of having control. And, if I decided that I was failing to meet their goals, I might become disappointed and possibly even defeated.

That Easter day when I imploded, I remember my parents' reaction. They were sorry that I was emotional and upset, but it gave them an opportunity to share with me what I have filed in my brain as a parenting tip for future use. Yes, I was difficult at times (I added the "at times" so that I'd feel better). "But," my dad explained, "when you are a parent your job is to 'do what it takes' for each one of your kids." And that is what they did. It took more energy and effort in the areas of disciplining me and teaching me godly self-control. "Do what it takes" meant other things for my brothers. That is part of what it takes to work together as husband and wife, as a team, to guide the journey of your strong-willed child. Set goals, determine your desired destination, and celebrate with one another (not with your child) as you and he reach those goals.

A Good Word from John, the Resident Dad

I have had a lot of goals in my lifetime, but none I pursued with more gusto than the goal of doing what it took to help each of our kids sing his song. I believe that God has put a song inside every individual. When someone sings their song, and sings it to God, that is my definition of glorifying God.

When I reflect on the goals that Kendra and I set for ourselves in regard to Aaron's development into responsible adulthood, I wish I would have had the skills, motivation, and, most of all, the knowledge I have today. I would like to have a "do-over"—or should I say an "add-on"—in that matter.

There is a paradox involved in parenting as it relates to spiritual growth. Hands-on parenting lasts only eighteen years. Spiritual growth goes on and on. We need to continually grow in our knowledge and love of God, but the knowledge gained after the kids are gone cannot help us in our parenting. In those limited years as mom and dad we do not know what we *will* know down the road.

With all the things I have learned since Aaron's early years, would I change the goals we had? No, I would simply augment them a bit. I would not change our primary goal to help Aaron know the love of God and accept Christ as his Savior. But I would not stop at that. I would do all I could to help Aaron understand the importance, responsibility, and privilege of becoming a disciple. It is not just a matter of checking something off on a "to do" list; it is making Jesus Lord and the treasure of your life.

That is what I have been learning as the years have progressed. I am no longer a hands-on dad, but through the grace of God, I still have the opportunity to share my life and my spiritual growth with Aaron and his brothers.

Take heart, Mom or Dad, as you grow in your relationship with the Lord you will undoubtedly realize things you "could have done better." God is grace-filled and the chances are your child is, too. If you didn't set your goals for parenting high enough, or if your goals were not met, know that God is not done with your child even if that child is now approaching adulthood.

And He is not done with you either.

"Maturity is when the child knows himself, accepts himself, controls himself, and is able to use what he is and has creatively and constructively."[5]

WARREN WIERSBE

CHAPTER SEVEN

The Journey Goes On:
High School

I'm not all that I ought to be,
but I thank God I'm not what I used to be.
If I keep praying and asking God to make me to be
what He wants me to be, some day I will be what I need to be . . .
in my walk with the Lord, I'm not saying I'm better than others—
I'm just better than I was.[1]

FRANCES KELLEY

As you already know, by high school great progress was made in the area of helping Aaron bring out the best in his strong-willed nature, but the journey was not complete. Aaron was assuming more and more responsibility for his decisions. And more and more of those decisions were very good ones.

His errant B grade in an easy course first semester of his freshman year was not repeated. He began to understand the personalities, quirks, and demands of his various teachers and of others with authority over him. He actually tried to function in their established parameters rather than his own. Helping your child realize that people have different personalities with varying strengths and weaknesses will help him to work with those individuals rather than be combative. It is also important to acknowledge the fact that aging does not equal maturing. Too often the strong-willed child cannot understand why an adult would act with immaturity. The answer is simple—some are not mature. By dialoging about this truth, you have freed your strong-willed child to accept the possibility of immaturity and to rise above the occasion.

Aaron found his academic niche in the areas of science and social science, two interests of his since childhood. He loved chemistry. Was this child really mine? (When I sat in an orientation session for the University a few years later, I heard a college chemistry professor explain that chemistry is really problem solving. Interesting. No wonder Aaron liked it so much.) Civics and political science were fascinating to him and fed his love of politics. Those teachers too appreciated his ability and propensity to think outside the box, making their classes even more enjoyable for Aaron.

> *"While great brilliance and intellect are to be admired, they cannot dry one tear or mend a broken spirit. Only kindness can accomplish this."*[2]
>
> JOHN M. DRESCHER

They enjoyed his questions and took time to answer them, encouraging Aaron to problem solve and dig deeper into the areas that interested him.

What kind of questions does your strong-willed child ask? The answer to that question might give you a clue about his interests, passions, and intellectual strengths. Then you can find ways to encourage and develop those interests and passions.

Of course, not everyone appreciated Aaron's questions. He ran into at least one coach who didn't want any questions at all and made that known by ridiculing Aaron when he asked one. Aaron's interest in that sport was definitely squelched, which, by the way, was NOT football. Football and Aaron were a perfect match! I always claimed that it was a wonderful channel for controlled aggression. Being aggressive was a necessary part of success in the game, which provided an outlet for him. I've known of other strong-willed children who participated in the martial arts. And sometimes simply providing a place where your strong-willed child can freely run will do the trick. Physical activities serve as a release for some of the strong emotions possessed by your strong-willed child.

Music was also an attraction and a talent that Aaron was able to cultivate with the loving attention of the directors of both the band and chorus. His high school was not very large, a little more than four hundred students, and the athletic and music departments discovered how to work together and share those teenagers interested in both endeavors. During his senior year, Aaron was one of the cocaptains of the football team and also one of the drum majors for the marching band. How did he do it? At halftime he removed his shoulder pads and climbed onto the director's stand. When the show was complete, he headed for the locker room. It was the best of both worlds! (And, as I said, it was a very small high school.)

Football and Aaron were a good match. Basketball and Aaron were not. Basketball, in fact, became an activity that Aaron chose to give up in order to have his way. He knew that we thought that there were positive things to be gained from participating in the sport. He also knew that we did not think it was an absolute necessity. Aaron was not a basketball star, but he had good fundamental skills that he had potential to build upon and have fun with. But Aaron wasn't willing to work; he wasn't willing to give it a try.

Sometimes the negative results of a decision don't manifest themselves immediately. That's what happened with basketball. After two years of participation in high school, he wanted to stop playing. We allowed him to make the choice not to be involved in it. And we knew that it probably was not a good choice and one he would regret. (See Aaron's comments on this decision at the end of the chapter.) But it is important to allow your child to make choices, especially if they are not a matter of life and death. Bad choices can teach lessons. There did not have to be any consequences imposed by us for Aaron's decision; the decision itself created the logical consequences. We knew that we were not in the business of raising basketball players but in the business of helping our strong-willed child reach maturity as a man of good character.

> "A life of obedience is not a life of following a list of do's and don'ts, but it is allowing God to be original in our lives."[3]
>
> VONETTE Z. BRIGHT

One of the biggest conflicts Aaron encountered in high school was definitely a result of his strong-willed nature, but it was his strong-willed nature under control and used for good! Aaron used his strong will as a wonderful asset by directing it in a positive way.

During his senior year, Aaron was the president of the local chapter of the Fellowship of Christian Athletes (FCA). They met every other Wednesday evening in the basement of a local business. When Aaron's senior year began, he requested that a notice of the meeting be put into the school announcements. His request was denied, stating that the school did not highlight any activities that were not specifically associated with academics. Was that response accurate? Not really. At the same time that the FCA announcements were NOT being read, announcements about teen dances at the American Legion and applications available for babysitting opportunities were read. "Hmmm," Aaron wondered, "how were local teen dances and babysitting specifically associated with academics?"

After consulting us, he contacted the Center for Law and Justice and discussed his situation with a lawyer who was on staff. This gentleman assured him that the school could not deny his announcement if it was including others that were outside the realm of academics. Aaron and his vice president, Jackie (the same young lady who had declared him smarter than the teacher during the coup incident), began to collect copies of the daily announcements, gathering evidence for their claim.

The lawyer sent Aaron booklets containing the pertinent laws and various legal interpretations. Enough booklets were received to potentially distribute to each administrator and every member of the board of education, which included his very own father. John was serving on the school board at that time. As we perused the information, it was very clear that the school was in the wrong for denying the inclusion of FCA announcements. There was truly no gray area because of the other announcements they allowed.

Interestingly enough, we already knew that the school did not include the FCA announcements before Aaron brought it to our attention. Matthew was FCA president two years before. When Matthew asked for their announcements to be included, his request was also denied. The difference was that he did not think it was a battle worth fighting. He just found an alternate way to get the word out to the students. When John began his first term on the school board a year later, he determined that the refusal to make FCA announcements was not the most pressing problem to address. So the issue was on hold until Aaron brought it up. "It is not fair. It is not right. In fact, it is not legal for the administration to deny the rights of the FCA organization," he declared. Aaron was right, and John could not deny it. This became an issue that would be brought by John to the school board.

Sometimes I lose sleep because of my vivid imagination. In this case, I could just imagine the possible headlines in the local paper—

School Board Member's Son Sues School! Yikes! I wished that Aaron and the administration had not come to loggerheads, but Aaron was right to stand up and demand that the law be followed. I recall that I had a few fitful nights' sleep until the school board, without Aaron's even attending a meeting, ruled to allow the FCA to participate in the school announcements. It was a battle that Aaron fought (with the help of his father) and won. And he did it with maturity and integrity. Very few people ever knew that it was a battle, only the two or three student leaders of FCA, their parents, the administration, school board, and school lawyer. When it was said and done, it was a victory, not just for Aaron or for the local FCA chapter, but also for the rights of Christian organizations—rights that are often ignored by others.

> "Some men march to the beat of a different drummer; and some polka."[4]
>
> ANONYMOUS

Have you ever wondered if standing up for what is right, even in the face of strong and powerful opposition, is the right thing to do? Does it make a difference? At the end of the year, at senior awards night, Aaron received the Principal's Award for leadership. (She obviously observed something she appreciated.)

One of the characteristics of a strong-willed child is an intense degree of loyalty. This manifested itself in varying ways throughout the years. In high school, when one of his female friends who was insecure in a particular area came under unfair attack from a teacher, Aaron was quick to defend her by attacking her attacker—verbally, of course. It wasn't the best decision, and, several apologies later, Aaron seemed to be back on track. The attribute of loyalty was manifest in an extreme way, which ended up being the wrong way. But that was happening with less frequency.

Another strong-willed characteristic is the courage to take chances. Aaron was not afraid of the unfamiliar and had a degree of confidence to try new things that exceeded many of his peers. The most obvious example occurred when he determined that he would try a new summer job, rather than repeat his former one in an office cubicle, trapped with an adding machine and a ledger sheet at the local CPA. He purchased an ad in the *Thrifty Nickel* and launched his own business, A & L Horses. The "A" was for Aaron, and the "L" was for Lady, the horse his grandfather purchased for him during the summer before fourth grade. He had no guarantee that anyone would be interested in having him "break and train horses" or "give beginning riding lessons," but he wanted to give it a try.

With college right around the corner, Aaron was aware of his need to generate income that summer, and he was sure he could do it in the horse business. A & L Horses was an extension and expansion of what he had begun years earlier with his encourager Ed. But now he had the advertisement of a sign at the end of our lane, business cards, and stationery. Not bad for an eighteen-year-old risk-taking entrepreneur. I still remember Matthew going to work that summer and wondering out loud why Aaron didn't have to work. Aaron discovered the key. Find something you like to do. Find someone who will pay you to do it, and you'll never "work" another day in your life.

"The two most important things we give to our children are roots and wings."
UNKNOWN

How about your strong-willed child? Where can you allow him to take chances that are not a matter of life and death? What encouragement can you give your strong-willed child to try something intriguing though unknown? Confidence is a terrific attribute that you can applaud.

A Closer Look with Aaron

My dad loves basketball. He was a very successful high school coach when he was teaching school. And he could see that I had the potential to do well and enjoy participating in the sport. But I didn't want to do it, because it was an activity that I didn't originally choose. There was no doubt in anyone's mind that I decided that I didn't like basketball. It must have been hard on him, but to his credit, he let me make the decision whether or not to stick with it. Actually, I was shocked! I chose to stop playing after my sophomore year. It was a bad choice, and I even knew it at the time. It didn't matter though; I wanted control. I quit for the satisfaction of being in control. I know this is difficult for anyone who is not strong-willed to understand, but, trust me, it is how we strong-willed people think.

My dad could have made me do it, but he didn't. With the freedom to choose came the responsibility for my actions and, in this case, the disappointment. Up to that point, I was seldom disappointed in my own behavior, even though my parents were at times. Now I was given the opportunity to make the decision, and I was responsible for my choice. Before, it always seemed that the result (in many cases the punishment) was the consequence of someone else's decision. I didn't completely make the association between my actions and the ultimate outcome. Because of that disassociation, I could be angry with someone else, typically the person delivering the consequences. With this particular decision, I could only be angry with myself.

What actually happened was that my parents allowed me to make a poor choice. I was allowed to fail. It was all my responsibility. I realize that this is a delicate dance for most parents. Obviously, no parent wants to see his child fail, but allowing failure is unbelievably important in the journey toward maturity. I'm not advocating that control of each and every choice should be given to your strong-willed child. That would be irresponsible.

Instead it is more like this: A young child sees a shiny knife on the counter, and he begs and cries for control of that "pretty thing." Of course, the responsible parent does not give in to those tears. As the child grows older, the parent teaches the child about the potential hazards of a knife and also gives him instructions about how to use it safely. Ultimately, the child is allowed to use a knife. The odds are that the trained young person will not do permanent damage to himself or something else. He might, however, be responsible for an occasional nick or cut. Do you see the analogy? You want to protect your child from harm until he is adequately instructed and able to understand the consequences of a mistake. Then you give him the responsibility to suffer the consequences or to enjoy the rewards of his own decisions. You see, it is twofold. The strong-willed child who is never allowed to fail is not only protected from disappointment, he is also sheltered from the positive results of his decisions.

As far as the incident with the Fellowship of Christian Athletes, that was a real adventure! Again my parents made the choice to allow me to pursue this matter. I am sure that being on the board of education made the possible confrontation very awkward for my dad. In a sense, he chose whether to remain comfortable or to face possible attack. In my black-and-white way of thinking, his choices were to (1) do what was right or (2) ignore the issue. So obviously, in my opinion, there was really no choice at all. There was only one correct answer. I am grateful that Dad made the "right" choice. I really think I'd still be mad today if he had not. After all, it was a legal issue and not just my opinion. But what about a different issue that your strong-willed child determines is important but is not as obvious and not a legal matter? When that is the case, you must make the decision about whether or not to allow your strong-willed child to pursue the concern. You must use clear-cut reasoning. It is important to be logical, honest, and compelling. Your own comfort will not be deemed an appropriate or persuasive reason to avoid the potential conflict. Remember, your strong-willed child is constantly on the lookout for people of character who stand for what is right. Be sure that you fall into that category.

It is true that high school was a critical time for me as I learned to respond to situations rather than react to them. I was coming to grips with the truth that I had the option of choosing or NOT choosing to try and control a situation. Furthermore, I was aware of the fact that there were things I couldn't control. And I was learning that I could always choose to control myself.

A Good Word from John, the Resident Dad

It was difficult enough to be the newly elected school board member. But within a few months I was to discover that it was even more difficult to be the newly elected school board member who, in the eyes of the administration, had a kid who was causing trouble.

The truth of the matter was that Aaron was not trying to cause trouble. You probably recall the story of Aaron's mission to get the Fellowship of Christian Athletes on the school announcements. He was trying to fix a problem, a problem that most people would have ignored. After he received permission to contact the Center for Law and Justice and read the material they sent, it was obvious that he was on firm legal ground. The school administration was denying the students in the Fellowship of Christian Athletes their constitutional rights.

During conversations with the lawyer, Aaron was asked if he would like to bring suit against the school district. As exciting and justified as that might have seemed, Aaron declined the offer, at least for the time being. "A lawsuit isn't necessary," he explained, "as long as we can put the FCA meeting times in the school announcements."

I remember the night that this issue was on the agenda for the board of education. I was asked point-blank if Aaron was planning to sue. My answer was an evasive one which caused an increased degree of tension in the boardroom. That tense atmosphere was topped off by comments from the district's lawyer who was present. The discussion went on for some time, and the attorney was asked for his professional opinion. After he had spoken, it was obvious that it was time to settle the issue in Aaron's favor. Aaron's request was granted.

The school board did the right thing. Much more important than that was the fact that Aaron knew that I was willing to "do the right thing." Aaron had made a good decision and it was my job to support him.

Building my relationship with Aaron was very important and has had positive long-term consequences. But more important than my relationship with Aaron, Kendra, or our other sons, is my obedience in my relationship with the Lord.

Pleasing Him should be our primary goal, even when that does not please others.

CHAPTER EIGHT

Encouragers and Discouragers

Where seldom is heard,
a discouraging word.
And the skies are not cloudy all day.[1]
BREWSTER HIGLEY, "HOME ON THE RANGE"

Wouldn't it be wonderful if those words from the song "Home on the Range" were completely accurate? Such a blessing if we seldom heard or said a discouraging word? Yes, it would be, but it is not reality. All of us have encountered, and been responsible for, discouraging words. And it is quite possible that strong-willed children have heard more discouraging words than their compliant counterparts. That possibility goes back to one of the assumptions vs. actualities—the incorrect assumption that these children are tough not tender. Because we have already discussed and debunked that assumption, we are aware that the discouragement faced by a strong-willed child is often taken to heart. Likewise, the encouragement that he receives will endear a strong-willed child to the encourager, potentially for a lifetime.

Aaron has a long list of people whom he would classify as encouragers and, thankfully, a shorter list of discouragers in his life. You have already met many of the people who would appear on these lists. You have been introduced to encouragers and discouragers. Rather than repeat those introductions, let's take a look at the common denominators. What traits and characteristics are shared, first of all, by the list of encouragers?

The most obvious shared quality is that these people did not embrace the assumptions typically made about a strong-willed child. For whatever reason, these folks saw the strong-willed nature for what it really is—a positive attribute. And they also realized that, like every other strength, it had to be controlled to be most effective. As I gazed at the list of encouragers, I was able to notice another generalization. Although the ages, professions, genders, political affiliations, and religious beliefs varied, all of the people who made the list of encouragers were "real." They did not pretend to be something they were not—they did not live a lie. Instead, they were mature and secure in themselves. They had nothing to prove, especially by demeaning or discouraging a child.

> *"Influence often isn't noticed until it blossoms later in the garden of someone else's life. Our words and actions may land close to home, or they may be carried far and wide."[2]*
>
> PAM FARREL

Are there people like that who can intersect with your strong-willed child? Yes, there are. Look for adults who are ready, willing, and able to let your strong-willed child know that he is loved. Find individuals who realize the potential of your child, recognize his talent, and appreciate his out-of-the-box thinking. Discover the people who will show respect for him and take him seriously—those who deserve and demand his respect.

What were the common denominators in the list of discouragers? In general, the discouragers believed the lies. They accepted one or more of the incorrect assumptions about a strong-willed child. For one reason or another, they did not take the time to search for the truth and apply it.

"As a nonconformist throughout high school, I was left with a deflated sense of self-worth and ended up in a relationship that further eroded my self-esteem. It has been a long, tough journey, but with the help of God and certain individuals that could see my gifts, I now have a loving marital relationship, three great kids (one of which is a strong-willed child—the middle one), and an appropriate sense of self. I am college educated, have a good job, am a

leader in my church, and am becoming a mentor to other women. I champion my strong-willed child's cause, having recently taken on her school principal in her defense. I don't want her to suffer the way I did."

In general, the list of discouragers contained people who were irritated and bothered by the unconventional thinking of a strong-willed child. They manifested this annoyance by frustration and disrespect. In some cases, discouraging adults actually teased and provoked Aaron. These discouragers tended to underestimate his skills and abilities and viewed his strong-willed nature as a liability rather than an asset. In general, those who made this list were insecure and lacked the maturity that one hopes comes with adulthood. Remember, just getting older does not make a person more mature.

> *"God does not dispense strength and encouragement like a druggist fills your prescription. The Lord doesn't promise to give us something to take so we can handle our weary moments. He promises us Himself. That is all. And that is enough."[3]*
> CHARLES SWINDOLL

> *For we are to God the aroma of*
> *Christ among those who are being saved*
> *and those who are perishing.*
> *To the one we are the smell of death;*
> *to the other, the fragrance of life.*
> 2 CORINTHIANS 2:15–16

Peers have an influence on children and adults alike. Again, Aaron could list encouraging peers and discouraging ones. But more than by reaction to his strong-willed nature, these two groups were polarized because of Aaron's faith and their faith (or lack of it). The encouragers usually shared Aaron's love for Jesus, and the discouragers found it distasteful.

For the most part, family members were encouragers to Aaron. What about his brothers? In Aaron's case, Matthew and Jonathan were and are encouragers. In order to understand that phenomenon and to make an attempt to foster those dynamics in your own home, several concepts need to be presented and understood.

First of all, sibling rivalry is a possibility in any home. However, there are things that you can do to reduce the risk of its development. Rivalry implies competition. One of your missions should be to eliminate competition between your children as much as possible.

I know of a set of twins who were continually pitted against one another in competitive ways. Before they could even walk, their father would put them at one end of the living room, stand at the other end, and have them crawl and race to him. And, destructively, he would then declare a "winner" and a "loser." By the time the twins were college graduates, they were, for all practical purposes, enemies. How sad!

In addition to eliminating competition whenever possible, it is also important to acknowledge that everyone has faults. Realizing that is a great help in developing and maintaining any human relationship. Shortcomings are not an excuse for misbehavior, but they are an opportunity to extend grace. I have always told the boys to allow at least three glaring faults in any individual. That practice greatly aids their ability to get along with others, even in their own family.

> *"Brotherly love is still the distinguishing badge of every true Christian."*[4]
> MATTHEW HENRY

Encouraging siblings to applaud each other's achievements is also an important deterrent to sibling rivalry. To this day, I hear Aaron bragging about the accomplishments of his brothers and vice versa. And in a family, there is a definite connection and correlation between accomplishments and family dynamics. The others in that family influenced one member's victory.

This leads me to a question that I am frequently asked: "Do you think my other children are negatively affected by having a sibling who is strong-willed?" Time after time, my answer to that question is emphatically, "No. Simply having a strong-willed family member is not a negative factor." Every single family has their own dynamics, and each member contributes to the whole package. Does a strong-willed child "ruin" the family dynamics? No, not any more than any other family member does. Let me give you an example by introducing you to a family I know.

Greg and Joan have two children. They are two years apart. Phillip is the older child and Elizabeth his younger sister. The dynamics of their particular family were not affected by one of the children being strong-willed. Instead it was something much more dramatic. Within hours of Elizabeth's birth, the doctor announced that she was profoundly mentally retarded. Today, at twenty-two years of age, Elizabeth is unable to walk, talk, or personally meet her basic daily needs. Yet I have never once heard her parents ask, "Do you think Phillip is negatively affected by having a sibling who is profoundly mentally retarded?"

Elizabeth needed, and actually still needs, more time and energy than Phillip. She is definitely more of a daily challenge. But she contributes to making their family what it is. Elizabeth influences the very nature of their family unit. And her parents would be the first to tell you that her influence is positive.

I specifically asked Matthew about how he interpreted the impact of having a brother who was strong-willed. And I quote some of his responses:

"I only felt deprived or negatively affected by it when we practiced basketball. Aaron took more than his share of time and attention, because he didn't want to practice. I *did* want to, and he distracted Dad. That affected my fun . . .

"As far as discipline, I never thought he was disciplined unfairly (although sometimes I wanted to be involved in the judiciary process). He deserved to be spanked! I enjoyed making sure he got punished, but, ironically, I felt bad when it actually happened . . .

"Sometimes I was embarrassed for him, wondering why having control was so important . . . important enough to alienate other people. I liked to be liked, so it was hard to understand . . .

"The summer after my senior year in high school we took a big family vacation to Alaska, and during that time it dawned on me that it was great to have Aaron around. We had actually become friends . . .

"It was obvious to me that Aaron and I didn't think the same way, but by the time I was ending high school, and definitely when we were both in college, I realized that it was good to be strong-willed. He was confident and could accomplish things the average person could never do!"

So what about your family? Does the fact that your strong-willed child is more high maintenance than his siblings negatively affect your family? It certainly doesn't have to if you are realizing the blessing you have been given in this particular child, this gift from God. There *may* be a negative influence on your family, however, if you have failed to avoid some of the roadblocks and detours along the way. There are several potential hazards that can turn your family dynamics upside down.

One of those obstructions is believing that you must deal with each child in your family equally. What? Isn't that the right thing to do, to make everything equal? No, equality is not the key; it is equity. Equity implies justice, fair play, and impartiality. Equality is uniformity and sameness. I have yet to meet two children whom I can treat with complete uniformity. Why? It is because no two children, strong-willed or not, are exactly the same. Equity in a household does not mean cookie-cutter responses from the parents. The compliant child probably does not require the consistent parental monitoring that a younger or older strong-willed child requires. Likewise, a strong-willed child may not be reprimanded in one arena or another because of the desire of the parent to choose the battles wisely.

Another potential rut in the journey of your strong-willed child is to allow his siblings to make him the scapegoat in all circumstances. Jonathan, Aaron's younger brother, learned from his oldest brother at a very early age to declare, "Aaron did it," whenever it might seem applicable. Did Aaron "do it"? Well, if I were a gambler, I would go with "yes." Did Aaron *always* "do it" when he was accused by his brothers? Absolutely not! Don't allow your strong-willed child to take the rap unfairly. This will alienate him from you and his siblings.

In the same way, avoid the peril of disciplining every one of your children when the discipline should only be directed to the strong-willed child. Many times the convoluted thinking is that if the siblings share the responsibility of the others' good behavior and share the punishment with the guilty strong-willed child, then they will apply positive "peer/sibling pressure." I suppose that could happen, but the parent who gives a blanket punishment to all involved runs the risk of polarizing the children. It makes them not only frustrated with the discipliner, but also very angry with their strong-willed sibling. The

> *"Life affords no greater responsibility, no greater privilege, than the raising of the next generation."*[5]
>
> C. EVERETT KOOP

chances of constructive adult relationships between siblings later in life diminish.

And finally, here is a roadblock that I encountered and needed to overcome. Since our other two sons were not strong-willed, I would ask them to do a certain task, because I knew it would not be a battle. I avoided asking Aaron to do his share of the family chores, ones he should have been expected to do, because I didn't want to engage in combat. This kind of behavior by a parent, if it goes uncorrected, can definitely cause the siblings of a strong-willed child to be negatively affected.

The key to fostering sibling love and encouragement is to be aware of the possible deterrents and to adjust and make corrections when they are needed. Remember, it is not a liability to your other children to be the brother or sister of a strong-willed child, unless you are failing to avoid roadblocks in the journey.

Never underestimate the power of your encouragement in the life of your strong-willed child. It is vital to your strong-willed child's well-being and successful journey. So, in a practical sense, what form should your encouragement take? Every parent can potentially apply the strengths of our original list of encouragers at the beginning of this chapter. The difference is that your intersection in the life of your child has more longevity, demands more patience and consistency, and is more important than any other person's contribution. Now is the time to remind you of the magnitude of the positive influence of your loving discipline. Never doubt the extent of your example—what you are modeling with your life. Always keep in mind that your strong-willed child is a gift from God, a gift whose possibilities are limitless. That is the mind-set of an encouraging parent.

Look for opportunities to encourage responsibility, to help your strong-willed child realize his significance in your family and ultimately in the world. For Aaron, we were able to encourage him in his love of animals. Lady, the horse, was a noteworthy encourager in her own right. Likewise, we surrounded Aaron with caring adults and included him in meaningful conversations with them as soon as he was able. We were very fortunate to have a supportive extended family. Aaron's grandparents, who live less than two miles away, were hands-on encouragers to him as were his other grandmother and relatives from Iowa to Indiana to Tennessee. They supported Aaron and applauded his abilities and talents. We believed that God had a special plan for Aaron. And we believed that He would "carry it on to completion until the day of Christ Jesus" (Philippians 1:6). We believed in Aaron, and he knew we believed in him. Do you believe in your strong-willed child? Does he know you believe in him?

> "When we pray, it is far more important to pray with a sense of the greatness of God than with a sense of the greatness of the problem."[6]
>
> EVANGELINE BLOOD,
> WYCLIFFE BIBLE TRANSLATOR

Inevitably, we also made mistakes. That is an unavoidable part of the human experience. Rather than allowing that potential roadblock to paralyze you in your parenting, the key is to make corrections for your mistakes whenever possible, as soon as possible.

By far the most important thing we did as the parents of a strong-willed child (or any child for that matter) was to pray. We prayed for Aaron and about Aaron. We asked for patience, wisdom, guidance, and blessings. And we listened and read the instruction book for parenting and life in general, the Bible.

In a very real sense, the potential encouragers and discouragers of a strong-willed child have varying degrees of influence based on their relationship to that child. We have been climbing the ladder of impact. Less significant are those people outside of your own home who intersect the life of your child. More influential are his extended family members, then his siblings, and finally, his parents. By far, the most powerful and positive encouraging influence can be found in your strong-willed child's relationship with the Lord, something you can influence through your relationship with God.

I've said it before and I'll say it again, parenting any child is not easy. And a strong-willed child is not just any child. Being the parent of a strong-willed child requires more patience, more persistence, more consistency, more wisdom, more knowledge, and more understanding. There is no formula, biblical or otherwise, to guarantee that your strong-willed child's journey will be a successful one to adulthood. But realizing and communicating to your child his value in God's eyes, helping your strong-willed child internalize the overflowing love that God has for him, and acknowledging the fact that God has a purpose and plan for his life can contribute to the journey toward responsible adulthood.

"A demanding spirit, with self-will as its rudder, blocks prayer . . . Prayer is men cooperating with God in bringing from heaven to earth His wondrously good plans for us."[7]

CATHERINE MARSHALL

A Closer Look with Aaron

It was interesting for me to reflect on the various individuals who positively and negatively affected my life. In some ways it was difficult because the discouragers stirred up some painful memories. It never ceases to amaze me that I can bring to the surface feelings from incidents that occurred so many years ago. One of the realities of being strong-willed is that your emotions are more intense—both positive and negative ones. When my older brother and I compare "war wounds" from our high school days, I realize that it took a lot more effort to inflict pain on him than it did for me. He tended to analyze the facts of an interaction while I reacted to the emotion behind it. These intense emotions that a strong-willed child feels can be rough on his parents.

I remember one particular example from my early high school days. It was summer, and I had gotten a new horse to break and train. He was a paint horse, and I named him Pablo Picasso, in honor of his modernistic coat. He was also the most stubborn horse I ever encountered. He absolutely refused to move in a forward direction. After I saddled him and mounted the saddle, he would back up until he finally backed into something (usually our machine shed), and then he would kick like crazy. His behavior baffled me. I'd never known a horse whose only gear was reverse. I tried this tactic and that tactic. And finally one night when I was completely out of strategies, I'd had it!!

I remember my mom coming out of our house, just when I had reached the end of my rope. I was completely deflated and discouraged by that silly horse. I was done with horse training, done with horseback riding, done with anything and everything that had to do with horses. It was obvious to me that I was a complete and utter failure in this department. With uncontrolled emotion, I poured out my frustration and pain to Mom. The next memory I have is the two of us sitting on top of the trampoline in our backyard. Mom was calmly and rationally discussing what things I might be able to do with Pablo Picasso. She reminded me of many other successes working with animals. And she generally soothed and comforted my wounded spirit. Somehow, in her words of kindness, she was able to encourage me not to quit but to try yet one more idea. She convinced me that I was NOT a failure, but I had merely determined the various training methods that would not work with this horse. (I think that's when she used the analogy of how many ways Edison had discovered NOT to invent the lightbulb.)

The result? My emotions were finally brought back under control, and I was encouraged that there was hope for me, for my horse skills, and for my small business. Encouragement is powerful. Encouragement from your parents is incredibly powerful. My mom thought I could be successful in my endeavors and genuinely believed that now was not the time to panic or give up. Did she have this great insight because of her equine knowledge and ability? Hardly! My mom knows horses have four legs and, well, actually, that might be about it! What she did know was that, with a little encouragement to combat the discouraging behavior of Pablo Picasso, her son could be successful.

Mom suggested to you earlier that because of the tender nature of a strong-willed child (and I would add because of the intensity of their emotions) they are easily hurt by discouragers and extremely loyal to their encouragers. That is true. Even today, if one of the teachers who made my list of encouragers called and needed for me to drop everything in order to do something for him or her, I would make every effort to do so. My appreciation and loyalty probably exceed the normal range, and I think that is true for all of us who have made the journey of a strong-willed child. I am very tuned in to the emotions and needs of those I love. My parents understood the powerful impact of encouragement, and our adult relationship reflects my appreciation of the safe home, the refuge, boundaries, and love they provided. The connection made with a strong-willed child is strong and lasting. It is all the more reason, it would seem, for the parent of such a child to strive to encourage and connect with him in positive ways.

The blessing of a strong-willed child is that she does everything with great passion. She loves her family with great passion and reminds us constantly of the good, both in her life and in ours.

A Good Word from John, the Resident Dad

As a parent, you have an astounding degree of influence in your child's life. The way you respond to different circumstances can affect your child's level of responsibility, his confidence, and even his faith. God's Word makes it clear that ours is a call to be an encourager. First Thessalonians 5:11: *"Therefore encourage one another and build each other up, just as in fact you are doing."*

Aaron's natural love of horses was one area where I could be an encourager to him, but I never imagined what that commitment would require of me. Encouragement is not just smiling and cheering and speaking a good word. Those things may be a part of it, but it is much, much more. I would learn that encouraging Aaron also involved risk and courage and trust.

Aaron loved horses long before he could say the word *thoroughbred*. It was definitely something God placed in his heart. He did not inherit it from me (although I grew up around horses on our farm) and he certainly didn't get it from Kendra.

Take a look at this series of events.

- At the age of 10, Aaron had his own horse.
- At the age of 14, he had two horses, a mare and a foal.
- At the age of 14, he had broken a stallion.
- At the age of 15, he made his first sale of a horse.
- At 16 he started his own business.
- At 18 he had trained over 35 horses and helped numerous kids learn how to ride.

This timeline is a wonderful illustration of a strong-willed child, transitioning into adulthood and investing his out-of-the-box ingenuity and energy in a positive direction.

Aaron's amazing endeavors were not done in a vacuum . . . back to that "risk and courage and trust" thing that God was calling me to as the dad of a strong-willed child.

Risk. There was risk involved in allowing Aaron to follow his dreams. I didn't necessarily want over thirty-five horses on our farm. These horses represented a potential financial risk. Aaron could not possibly afford to pay if an accident occurred. A young adult does not assume the financial risk. I knew it would be mine. Aaron wanted the responsibility for his own business where he was the boss, but I would have to be the one to allow the risk. The decision had to be made whether the return would justify the risk and whether the risk was one led by God.

Courage. I have come to learn that it takes courage to relinquish control. The question I had to ask myself was would I relinquish my control to Aaron. I believe that it is the responsibility of a parent to be a "student of his child." As the timeline indicated, I determined that Aaron was ready to be in control of more and more. God gave me the courage to give up a great deal of my hands-on parental control. That decision was a true confidence-builder for Aaron.

Trust. This calling was twofold. I had to trust Aaron's decisions when it came to working with the horses, with their owners, and managing his business. I would not be standing beside him, voting on or amending his judgment. And I had to trust my heavenly Father who is and was Aaron's heavenly Father, too. God would have to take care of one of my greatest treasures, my son.

Being an encourager is not always as simple as it sounds. But it is the instruction that God gives.

I would challenge you to take the risk, be courageous, and trust in the Lord as you encourage your strong-willed child.

CHAPTER NINE

It Goes On and On:
College and Beyond

Freedom is not the right
to do as a person pleases,
but the liberty to do as he ought.
CICERO

You are now hearing from me, Aaron. I am officially switching seats with my mom. Now I am in the driver's seat of my journey; Mom and Dad are just passengers. That's how it is when your kids reach eighteen. They are, for all practical purposes, adults. By the end of high school, I was ready to take the controls, and the folks seemed to be pretty comfortable with me at the helm. Comfortable or not, when your strong-willed child (or any other child, for that matter) graduates from high school, he is no longer a child.

At my high school graduation, there were many things to celebrate. I'd been accepted at the University of Illinois, majoring in animal science/pre-vet. I tried out for the Marching Illini and secured a spot in that prestigious marching band. I was going to live on campus in a fraternity with my older brother, Matthew. And the girl of my dreams was still in the picture. Those successes can all be attributed to the effort put into my ongoing strong-willed journey, a journey that never really ends but merely gets smoother and smoother.

College was a challenge that demanded the use of my strong-willed persistence. Needless to say, I was well trained in the area of perseverance, and it paid off. I set a goal of my own choosing. I wanted to get into vet medicine school. With the same tenacity I formerly applied to the less important areas of my life, I attacked this goal. I studied and worked hard to move toward my target of vet school. I remember the first time I thought that maybe I could actually achieve my objective. It was during the first week of classes. I went to college wondering if my academic preparation was adequate. Would I be able to compete with students from bigger schools, schools that had AP (advanced place-ment) classes and fancy lab equipment? I was nervous until it dawned on me that the professors spoke the same language that I did. I know it sounds silly, but somehow I imagined that I would not even be able to understand the lectures. When I realized that was a myth, I gave it my all. There was nothing to lose by working my hardest. And that is exactly what I did. School was a top priority—not the Marching Illini, not the fraternity, not even my girlfriend, Kristin. I was pursuing my goal with the diligence of a strong-willed individual.

The Marching Illini was, in one sense, a good diversion. I liked to play my horn, and being in the marching band certainly gave me that opportunity. In fact, it was very close to "too much of a good thing." We practiced two hours each day, Monday through Friday, and four hours on Tuesday. And then, of course, there were the games all day on Saturday. Plus, I spent a few hours practicing each week so that I would make the Thursday cut. Many times I questioned the wisdom of devot-ing long hours to something that wasn't directly a part of reaching my primary goal. Because of my strong-willed drive, however, I stayed with it and made the cut each week for the two years I played in the band. I suppose it was a positive break from my obsessive studying. Also, it pro-vided me with another link to my older brother. Matthew was a student coach for the football team, so we intersected even more. For me, the band was sort of a "brother thing."

So was the fraternity. I lived there only because he did. Neither one of us was a very committed Greek. In fact, the fraternity house gave me one last fling at over-the-top strong-willed behavior.

You see, there were some men in our fraternity house who were making very poor decisions. It was voted that our house would be "sub-stance free." That meant no tobacco, liquor, or drugs on the property. Unfortunately, a few guys decided to violate the rule and went as far as smoking pot in the house. That definitely stirred my sense of right and wrong. As far as I was concerned, it was a black-and-white issue (remember how I love those?). Something had to be done. I led the charge to have these men punished for their poor choices. In retrospect, I look back at the battle I fought, and to some degree won, and I question whether or not it was worth the fight. It took a great deal of time and alienated a lot of the guys. But I also developed some genuine, life-long friendships. The alienation didn't really matter to me, because I saw the goal as more important than their perception of me. By this time in my life, I was used to people jumping to conclusions about who I was and why I did what I did. Those conclusions were usually far from accurate. The two most significant people in my life at that point, my brother and my girlfriend, thought what I did was right, so I walked away from that battle with only a few minor scars.

I told you that I developed some solid friendships during my college years. Interestingly, they were friends that, for the most part, I shared with my older brother. When I reflected on that phenomenon, I realized that because of my rabid study habits, I spent little time exploring friendship possibilities. It was much easier to simply adopt the friends Matthew had already pre-classified and "broken in." That worked very well for me, and I appreciated the camaraderie. Unfortunately, it dawned on me at the beginning of my junior year that most of these friends had graduated and were gone.

My best friend, my girlfriend, Kristin, was still in school, but she attended another university about one hour away. My junior year was a lonely school year for me, but with academics as my primary focus, I had plenty of time to devote to that area. And that is exactly what I did. One of the things I always appreciated about Kristin was her willingness to take a backseat to my immediate goal of getting into vet school. Many dates were spent at the library or studying in the fraternity house. She was patient and supported my sometimes out-of-control preoccupation with my classes. To me that was love in action. I knew that having my classes as my primary focus was what it would take to get accepted to vet school, and she supported my dream.

And that was not the only thing Kristin knew about me. She was well aware of my strong-willed nature and shared the opinion that, when under control, it was a wonderful attribute. She had witnessed that "strength carried to extremes," and I guess (as my mother would say) that was one of the glaring faults she allowed. Interestingly, Kristin was in my grade school class the year that I organized the coup and took over. Even more interesting is the fact that she cannot remember the incident! Now that is love in the form of selective forgetfulness! Kristin's gracious spirit, her love of me and of Jesus endeared her to me more and more each day.

In October of my junior year I applied for early admission to vet school. And then I waited. Before too long, I received notice that I was granted an interview. This was a very significant step. Approximately four hundred students interviewed. Around one hundred students would be admitted. The day I was notified that I was officially a member of next year's class of first-year vet students I was ecstatic! My perseverance and persistence paid off. My determination and bulldog-focus led to success. My strong-willed nature was a tremendous asset and helped me reach a goal that I'd looked toward since third grade.

As I write this, I am a vet student. It is not easy. But it is the next step in my journey. I am also a husband. Kristin and I married in August before I began school. For a few years I had the encouragement and assistance of many, but I was primarily alone in my responsibility for making forward progress on my journey. Now Kristin and I are traveling together. My parents are and always will be supportive, but they no longer steer the journey nor determine the route. In my childhood they helped navigate. They lovingly disciplined and guided me. They cheered me on at every possible juncture. And they still support me with their prayers. Ultimately, every strong-willed child must travel alone. The key is to equip your child and prepare him for the time when you, his parents, will no longer be in the driver's seat. Your child will take control of the journey, something he has always longed to do.

A Closer Look with Kendra (Mom)

Wow, relegated to the comments on the chapter, things really do change. Every parent, one with a strong-willed child or otherwise, has the desire to work himself out of a job. From the very beginning, it was our hope to see Aaron mature into a capable, well-adjusted adult. We knew that once he was able to master control of his strong-willed nature that he would be able to use it for good. I have seen his tenacity in many arenas of life, like in his career pursuit, leadership, quest for what is right, love of others, and faith. I look back on the journey and realize that every battle chosen and won, every discussion of right and wrong, and every identification of his strengths being carried to extremes was worth the time and energy it demanded.

And I also realize that I am looking at these things in hindsight. The chances are great that you are presently in the infancy of the journey with your strong-willed child. You have no history to guide you, and no benchmarks to celebrate, at least not yet. Take heart. That is the reason that my husband, John, Aaron, and I have spent hours thinking, praying, writing, and rewriting. It is for you—for you and your strong-willed child. My desire is to hear from you many years from now, after your strong-willed child has reached adulthood. I hope to hear that you are no longer the parent of a strong-willed child but instead are the parent of a capable, well-adjusted adult.

A Good Word from John, the Resident Dad

I want to "amen" Kendra's words. What a treat to now have Aaron in the driver's seat for the journey. At this point in Aaron's life I have moved into an advisory role—an unpaid consultant. This shift to the backseat for the remainder of the journey is not a demotion. It is in every sense the spot we were hoping to ultimately occupy.

A few years ago my three sons gave me a very special Father's Day gift. It is a framed picture of a KC-135, the aircraft I flew in the Air Force and Air Force Reserves for almost thirty years. They had written a personal note directly on the print. "Thanks for the wings! Love, Matthew, Aaron, Jonathan."

Dads, it is an act of loving-kindness to give your kids, strong-willed and otherwise, roots and to give them wings.

The Rest of the Story (So Far . . .)

As the three of us worked on this project I often said that Aaron was the heart, John was the brains, and I was the voice. In my self-appointed role as the voice, I thought you might like to hear the update on our strong-willed child turned responsible adult.

Aaron graduated from the University of Illinois College of Veterinary Medicine in May of 2007. He and his wife, Kristin, live in Goshen, Indiana, where he practices medicine. They have an adorable daughter, Jenna Ruth. I LOVE this grandma thing! You might wonder if she is strong-willed. The jury is still out. Since you and I both know that being strong-willed can be a wonderful asset, it really doesn't matter, does it?

I truly believe that once strong-willed, always strong-willed. A year or two ago Aaron told me that the key is to know when to turn it off and when to turn it on. As a mom, it's great to see evidence of that maturity. As your strong-willed child matures, my desire is that the resource you hold in your hand serves you well. My expectation is that each chapter will encourage and equip you on your journey. I am almost certain it will give you hope for your personal *Journey of a Strong-Willed Child.*

Conclusion:
Do You See What I See?

We may run, walk, stumble, drive or fly,
but let us never lose sight
of the reason for the journey
or miss a chance to see
a rainbow on the way.[1]
GLORIA GAITHER

We have come to the conclusion. Not the conclusion of the journey, but the conclusion of the book. I have again taken over the pen as we bring this narrative to a close. The birthing of this book has brought me both pleasure and pain, much like the birthing of my children. And, just as most other mothers feel, the pleasure has overshadowed the pain. Joy remains long after the memory of discomfort has vanished.

As we were writing this book, Aaron was the teacher of the fourth and fifth grade Sunday school class at the church he and Kristin attended. One day he and another teacher were chatting about Aaron being strong-willed, and the conversation turned to this book. Aaron shared one or two stories, and the other teacher asked him a question that stymied him, at least momentarily. "How is it that you can be so introspective and so transparent?" Aaron told me about the interchange and said that at the time he had no answer. Then after some thought and prayer, he realized that it was really very simple. "I am able to share about my faults and how I stumbled in my journey because of the grace of God. I made mistakes and will undoubtedly continue to make mistakes, just like everyone else. We are all sinners saved by grace. Without

God's grace no one would be forgiven from strong-willed antics or compliant failings."

One Easter Sunday I heard a wonderful sermon at the little country church we attend. Our pastor preached on John 20:19–30, the story of doubting Thomas. Thomas demanded proof of Jesus' resurrection:

"Grace is the good pleasure of God that inclines to bestow benefits upon the undeserving."[2]
A.W. TOZER

"Unless I see the nail marks in his [Christ's] hands and put my finger where the nails were, and put my hand into his side, I will not believe it." Rather than dwelling on the doubt of Thomas, our pastor talked about the fact that Christ met with Thomas after the resurrection and *still* bore the scars of the crucifixion. Why wasn't the risen Lord in a perfect and whole body? It was because He was able to minister through His scars. And so are we. Everyone has scars and wounds from the journey of life. We usually choose to hide those blemishes from others and even try to ignore them ourselves. But God's grace empowers us to persevere through our journey, with all its roadblocks, bumps, setbacks, and detours. We can share the stories behind our scars in hopes that we can minister through them.

"Nothing we can do will make the Father love us less; nothing we do can make Him love us more. He loves us unconditionally with an everlasting love. All He asks of us is that we respond to Him with the free will that He has given to us."[3]
NANCIE CARMICHAEL

It is God's grace that enables us to be authentic and forgiven despite the fact that our lives have been fault-filled. Never underestimate the power of grace in your own life, the life of your strong-willed child, or the lives of those you intersect.

We have taken you through over twenty years of our journey. And, hopefully, you have been encouraged, challenged, and enlightened en route. Now I leave you to travel your own journey. But before this book is closed, and it comes to permanent rest on a shelf, let me share one final thought, beginning with a closer look with Jesus.

A Closer Look with Jesus

Matthew 4:18–20: As Jesus was walking beside the Sea of Galilee, he saw two brothers, Simon called Peter and his brother Andrew. They were casting a net into the lake, for they were fishermen. "Come, follow me," Jesus said, "and I will make you fishers of men." At once they left their nets and followed him.

Jesus was walking beside the Sea of Galilee. He saw two brothers, Simon called Peter and his brother Andrew. These two men were casting a net into the lake, a very logical thing for two fishermen to do. Undoubtedly Peter and Andrew looked like fishermen, smelled like fishermen, and their actions supported the notion that they were fishermen. If you and I were walking on the same path as Jesus, walking beside the Sea of Galilee, we would have seen these two brothers. We would have known that they were fishermen. We would have recognized the obvious.

> "If we love people,
> we will see them
> as God intends
> them to be."[4]
>
> FLORENCE LITTAUER

But Jesus saw something more. He saw beyond the obvious. His vision wasn't limited to the apparent. He saw all that you and I would see, but He also saw more. We would just see fishermen. Jesus saw disciples.

Look into the eyes of your strong-willed child. What do you see? Do you only see the obvious—the out-of-the-box thinker who is demanding and difficult? Do you just see an annoying child who is so "right" all the time?

> "Oh the comfort, the inexpressible comfort
> of feeling safe with a person; having neither
> to weigh thoughts nor measure words
> but to pour them all out, just as it is,
> chaff and grain together, knowing that
> a faithful hand will take and sift them,
> keeping what is worth keeping,
> and then, with the breath of kindness
> blow the rest away."[5]
>
> MARIAN EVANS CROSS (GEORGE ELIOT)

Ask God to help you see your child through His eyes. Look through the eyes of Jesus. You just might see a disciple.

Notes

Introduction—Aaron and Others

1. James Dobson, *The Strong-Willed Child* (Wheaton, Ill.: Tyndale House, 1978), 24.

2. Samuel Butler (1612–1680), *Hudibras* Part iii. Canto iii. Line 547, from *Familiar Quotes*, comp. John Bartlett, Familiar Quotations, 10th ed., rev. and enl. by Nathan Haskell Dole (Boston: Little, Brown, & Co., 1919).

3. LaHaye, *Spirit-Controlled Temperament* (Wheaton, Ill.: Living Studies, 1982).

4. Florence Littauer, *Personality Plus* (Grand Rapids, Mich.: F. H. Revell Co., 1992).

5. Corrie ten Boom, *A Woman's Journey with God* (Nashville, Tenn.: Brighton Books by Mary Prince, 2001), 21.

Chapter 1—The Journey Begins: Birth to Pre-Kindergarten

1. William Shakespeare (1564–1616), Launcelot, in *The Merchant of Venice*, act 2, scene 2, lines 72–73 (1600). "Launcelot repeats a proverbial saying as he attempts to make himself known to his blind father, Gobbo." *The Columbia World of Quotations.* (New York: Columbia University Press, 1996).

Chapter 3—The Journey Continues: Kindergarten to Grade Six

1. Shirley Dahlquist, my friend, deceased, former resident of Como, Colorado.

2. Sheila Walsh, from *Calendar—For a Woman's Heart: Thoughts by Women for Women* (Bloomington, Minn.: Garborgs, 1998, 1999).

3. Beth Moore, *A Woman's Journey with God* (Nashville, Tenn.: Brighton Books by Mary Prince, 2001), 110.

4. Norman Vincent Peale, from *Minute Motivators for Teachers*, ed. Stan Toler (Tulsa, Okla.: RiverOaks Publishing, 2002), 10.

Chapter 4—Assumptions vs. Actualities

1. Carol Lynn Mithers, "The Perils of the Pushover Parent," *Ladies' Home Journal* (January 2003) 92, 94–96.

2. Helen Keller, from *Calendar—For a Woman's Heart: Thoughts by Women for Women* (Bloomington, Minn.: Garborgs, 1998, 1999).

3. Elisabeth Elliot quote, ibid.

4. Cynthia Tobias, *You Can't Make Me* (Colorado Springs, Colo.: Waterbrook, 1999), 24.

5. Louis Pasteur, from *To Your Success*, comp. Dan Zadra (Edmonds, Wash.: Compendium, Inc., 1997), 78.

6. James Dobson, *The Strong-Willed Child* (Wheaton, Ill.: Tyndale House, 1978), 21.

7. Pamela Smith and Carolyn Coats, *Alive and Well in the Fast Lane* (Nashville, Tenn.: Thomas Nelson Publishers, 1994), 23.

8. Adolf Hitler, Announcement to the German Army of his assumption of its command, December 21, 1941. Originally published in the *New York Times*, December 22, 1941. Found at www.ibiblio.org/pha/policy/1941/411221a.html.

Chapter 5—The Junior High Journey

1. Wayne Rice, *Understanding Your Teen* (Nashville, Tenn.: Word Publishing, 1999), ix.

2. William Shakespeare (1564–1616), Falstaff, in *Henry IV*, Part 1, act 5, scene 4, lines 119–20. Falstaff's "discretion" meant avoiding danger on the battlefield by pretending to be dead. *The Columbia World of Quotations* (New York: Columbia University Press, 1996).

3. Wayne Rice, *Understanding Your Teen*, gathered from a seminar on this book.

Chapter 6—Determining the Desired Destination

1. *431 Quotes from the Notes of Henrietta C. Mears*, ed. Eleanor L. Doan (Glendale, Calif., G/L Regal Books, 1970).

2. "Patience," *The Music Machine*, 25 min. (Bridgestone Group: Agapeland Recordings, 1990), VHS videotape.

3. Theodore Roosevelt, from *God's Little Instruction Book for Teachers* (Tulsa, Okla.: Honor Books, 1999), 132.

4. EDGE Learning, *To Your Success*, comp. Dan Zadra (Edmonds, Wash.: Compendium, Inc., 1997), 19.

5. Warren Wiersbe, quoted in *Parents and Teenagers*, Jay Kesler with Ronald A. Beers (Wheaton, Ill.: Victor Books, 1984), 409.

Chapter 7—The Journey Goes On: High School

1. Frances Kelley, from "Better Than I Was," in *Quotable Quotes*, comp. Helen Hosier (Uhrichsville, Ohio: Barbour Publishing Co., 1998), 121.

2. John M. Drescher, from "Now Is the Time to Love," in *Quotable Quotes*, 81.

3. Vonette Z. Bright, from "For Such a Time as This," in *Quotable Quotes*, 161.

4. Quote from *To Your Success*, comp. Dan Zadra (Edmonds, Wash.: Compendium, Inc., 1997), 16.

Chapter 8—Encouragers and Discouragers

1. Brewster Higley, "Home on the Range," from *The Western Home* (Originally 1873). Modern version by John Lomax, who, on his first trip west, recorded a black saloon keeper in San Antonio singing "Home on the Range" on an Edison cylinder, and the lyrics were written down and published in the book "Cowboy Songs and Frontier Ballads" by Lomax in 1910. The song became a national favorite and is the state song of Kansas. Steve Schoenherr, University of San Diego Department of History. Found at http://history.sandiego.edu/gen/recording/notes.html. First published April 18, 1995; notes revised July 6, 2005.

2. Pam Farrel, from *Calendar—For a Woman's Heart: Thoughts by Women for Women* (Bloomington, Minn.: Garborgs, 1998, 1999).

3. Charles Swindoll, from "Encourage Me," in *Quotable Quotes*, comp. Helen Hosier (Uhrichsville, Ohio: Barbour Publishing Co., 1998), 58.

4. Matthew Henry, from "Moments of Meditation," in *Quotable Quotes*, 155

5. C. Everett Koop, from *Minute Motivators for Teachers*, ed. Stan Toler (Tulsa, Okla.: RiverOaks Publishing, 2002), 5.

6. Evangeline Blood, from *Quotable Quotes*, 176.

7. Catherine Marshall, from *Quotable Quotes*, 178. Originally published in *Adventures in Prayer* (Old Tappan, N.J.: distributed by F. H. Revell, 1975).

Conclusion—Do You See What I See?

1. Gloria Gaither, *Calendar—For a Woman's Heart: Thoughts by Women for Women* (Bloomington, Minn.: Garborgs, 1998, 1999).

2. A. W. Tozer, from *Quotable Quotes*, comp. Helen Hosier (Uhrichsville, Ohio: Barbour Publishing Co., 1998), 116. Originally published in A. W. Tozer, *Knowledge of the Holy* (San Francisco: HarperSanFrancisco, 1961).

3. Nancie Carmichael, *Calendar*.

4. Florence Littauer, from *Minute Motivators for Teachers*, ed. Stan Toler (Tulsa, Okla.: RiverOaks Publishing, 2002), 72.

5. Marian Evans Cross (George Eliot, pseud.) from *Quotable Quotes*, 90.

LIVE LIFE INTENTIONALLY!
This phrase describes Kendra's
life and the message that she brings
to her listening and reading audiences.
Kendra would be delighted to hear from you.
Contact her at: www.KendraSmiley.com

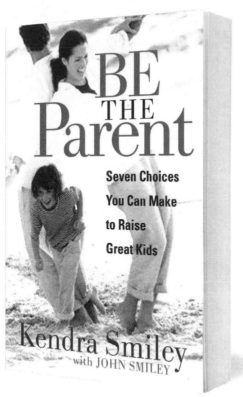

ISBN-13: 978-0-8024-6941-0

Instead of tuning in to *Super Nanny* or *Nanny 911*, pick up this humorous yet biblically solid book of parenting advice. Kendra Smiley, author of *High Wire Mom, Do Your Kids a Favor . . . Love Your Spouse,* and *Empowering Choices,* once again hits on a subject that moms and dads are longing to hear—how can I be a better parent and raise great and godly children? With wisdom gleaned both as parent and teacher, Kendra suggests seven proactive choices parents can make to help reduce family stress and avoid parenting emergencies. Each chapter ends with a dash of advice from her husband, John, who offers a dad's point of view. Whether exhausted and struggling or just longing to improve their skills, *Be the Parent* is the perfect resource for moms and dads seeking to positively impact their children. Includes survey responses from real parents. Visit www.ParentingLikeAPro.com.

by Kendra Smiley with John Smiley

Find it now at your favorite local or online bookstore.

Sign up for Moody Publishers' Book Club on our website.

www.MoodyPublishers.com

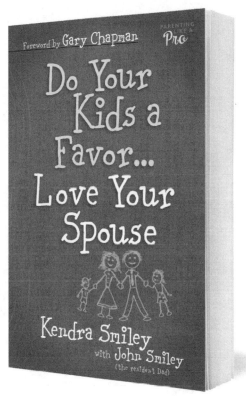

ISBN-13: 978-0-8024-6942-7

Building a healthy marriage can give your kids a great head start in life. Kendra and John Smiley learned this through the ups and downs of raising three sons, all now grown. With her trademark humor, honesty, and the wisdom that she has shared on *Focus on the Family* and *Family Life Today*, Kendra offers practical, day-in, day-out insights on kids, marriage, and much more. She shares her wisdom on such topics as setting priorities and coming to grips with family backgrounds, showing how when we make the right choice for our marriage, we're making the right choice for our children. "Resident Dad" John pitches in with his perspective. Learn how to "parent like a pro!" Visit www.ParentLikeAPro.com.

by Kendra Smiley with John Smiley
Find it now at your favorite local or online bookstore.

Sign up for Moody Publishers' Book Club on our website.

www.MoodyPublishers.com